The Nature of Revival

The Nature of Revival

Compiled, Edited and Abridged by Clare George Weakley, Jr.

JOHN WESLEY

CHARLES WESLEY & GEORGE WHITEFIELD

BETHANY HOUSE PUBLISHERS
MINNEAPOLIS, MINNESOTA 55438
A Division of Bethany Fellowship, Inc.

Published by Bethany House Publishers
A Division of Bethany Fellowship, Inc.
6820 Auto Club Road, Minneapolis, Minnesota 55438

Printed in the United States of America

Library of Congress Cataloging-in-Publication Data

Wesley, John, 1703-1791.
   The nature of revival.

   (The Wesley library for today's reader)
   Edited selections from the private journals of John and Charles
Wesley and George Whitefield.
    1. Wesley, John, 1703-1791—Diaries. 2. Wesley, Charles, 1707-
1788—Diaries. 3. Whitefield, George, 1714-1770—Diaries.
4. Methodist Church—Great Britain—Clergy—Biography.
5. Methodist Church—Great Britain—History—18th century.
6. Calvinistic Methodists—Great Britain—Clergy—Biography.
7. Calvinistic Methodists—Great Britain—History—18th Century.
8. Revivals—Great Britain—History—18th century. 9. Great Britain—Church history—18th century.
I. Weakley, Clare G. II. Wesley, Charles, 1707-1788. Selections.
1987. III. Whitefield, George, 1714-1770. Selections. 1987.
IV. Title. V. Series: Wesley, John, 1703-1791. Wesley library for today's reader.
BX8491.W382   1987   287'.092'2 [B]   86-31058
ISBN 0-87123-925-6

Dedication

This book is dedicated to
George Whitefield,
whose call, anointment, and dedication
cannot be duplicated.

JOHN WESLEY (1703–1791) was the founder of Methodism. Although raised in a godly home and trained for the ministry at Oxford, Wesley's failure as a missionary in Georgia (1735–1738) revealed his unsaved condition. Returning to England, he was soon converted and embarked on his lifework: "To reform the nation, particularly the Church, and to spread Scriptural holiness over the land." The organization of Methodism was the direct outcome of his success in preaching the gospel.

CHARLES WESLEY (1707–1788) is remembered as the "sweet singer" of Methodism. Accompanying John in their abortive mission to Georgia, Charles was converted three days before John. He joined John in the work of evangelism, eventually becoming one of the most powerful of the open-air preachers of the revival. He was also the most gifted and most prolific of all English hymnwriters—some 7,270 such compositions came from his pen.

GEORGE WHITEFIELD (1714–1770) attended Oxford and associated with those who formed the "Holy Club," through which he experienced conversion. He first discovered the effectiveness of open-air preaching and regularly delivered up to twenty sermons a week. Theological differences separated him from the Wesleys, but the results of their preaching was much the same. Many regard him as the supreme open-air preacher of all time.

CLARE WEAKLEY, JR. is a businessman, lecturer, and chaplain-at-large in his community. He received a B.B.A. and an M.Th. from Southern Methodist University. He is married and he and his family make their home in Dallas, Texas.

Editor's Remarks

This book brings gems of Christian history from obscurity into this era to help us grow in faith. Of necessity, all the works are both paraphrased and abridged for easy understanding. They are also lifted from their original contexts.

For those with more interest in Whitefield and the Wesleys and their writings, the original sources have been listed.

On completion of this third Wesley abridgement, my appreciation goes to several who contributed to it. Many thanks to Nathan Unseth, of Bethany House, who resurrected this idea and encouraged me to continue the Wesley series. Gratitude is extended to Murney Call who met Nathan's typing deadline and did the fine honing of the text. I also acknowledge the important assistance of Gene Barrett's photocopier, Anne Murchison's Epson word processor, and Jean Weakley's dining-room table. It was on the dining-room table that the ninety-day birthing and nurturing of this book took place. And, of course, appreciation to Bridwell Library for the use of its Wesley material and to Perkins School of Theology for what it did toward molding my way of thinking. The time spent earning my theology degree there was joyful and rewarding. Thankfully, my Lord and Savior sent me His Holy Spirit many years prior to my studies there.

Clare G. Weakley, Jr.
Dallas, Texas
September 1, 1986

The Wesley Library for Today's Reader

Preface

As Whitefield was one of the master-spirits who communicated to Methodism its first impulse and direction, a brief survey of the religious condition of that period, and the production of this sect from it, is highly pertinent to an account of it. At that time, serious and practical Christianity in England was in a very low condition. Scriptural, experimental religion, which in the last century had been the subject of the sermons and writings of the clergy, had become quite unfashionable. The only thing insisted on was a defense of the out-works of Christianity against the objections of infidels. What was the consequence? Writings of infidels multiplied every day, and infidelity made a rapid progress among persons of every rank, not because they were reasoned into it by the force of argument, but because they were kept strangers to Christ and the power of the gospel. We have a most affecting description of this, by Bishop Butler, "It is come, I know not how, to be taken for granted by many persons, that Christianity is not so much as a subject of inquiry; but that it is, now at length, discovered to be fictitious. Accordingly, they treat it as if in the present age this were an agreed point among all people of discernment, and nothing remained but to set it up as a principle subject of mirth and ridicule, as it were by way of reprisals for its having so long interrupted the pleasures of the world."

While pure and undefiled religion was well nigh extinct in England, and fast becoming so in Scotland, it pleased God to keep alive, in the persons of this despised Methodist band, that salt of the earth which was to save it from moral putrefaction. Its beginnings were so feeble as to be scarcely observable; but, like the mustard seed, it shot up into a mighty tree, whose branches now clasp, in greater or less degrees, all Christendom. John and Charles Wesley had, in good earnest, been religiously educated by parents who had been quickened by the Spirit of God, and manifested the fruits of it in sober and godly lives.

In the course of their education, God delivered them from conformity to the habits and feelings of an age of abounding impiety, by His super-abounding grace. John was the first to feel its renewing and quickening power, and to transfuse its spirit into the details of life and action. He sought to press upon his brother the importance of austerer habits, and a more active devotion, but found him too much imbued with the current notion of a gradual reformation of character to think of becoming a saint all at once. While, however, John was absent at Wroote, the process which he had been vainly endeavoring to accelerate in his brother was silently going on. His disposition, his early education, the example of his parents, and of both his brethren, all concurred toward a change, which he piously referred to his mother's prayers. Finding two or three fellow-students, including George Whitefield, whose inclinations and principles resembled his own, they associated together for the purpose of religious improvement, lived by rule and received the sacraments weekly. Such conduct would at any time have excited attention in an English University; it was peculiarly noticeable during the dreadful laxity of opinions and morals which then existed.

JOHN GILLIES, D.D.
Memoirs of Rev. George
Whitefield
(Hunt and Noyes)
Middletown, 1837

Table of Contents

Introduction

Two common myths about Methodism have caused many of the details of the greatest revival since Pentecost to be ignored. First, it is generally believed that Methodism and the Methodist church are the same. Second, many assume that John Wesley was only the founder of the Methodist church, even though the Wesleys were never members of it.

Rivals with no interest in studying the Methodist denomination are therefore derailed from learning about the eighteenth-century Methodist revival which ran forty-eight years before the Methodist church was ever created in America. That early revival and the denomination which followed are very different.

Early Methodism was a great charismatic revival that occurred outside the established churches and was opposed by most of them. This revival began under the anointed preaching of George Whitefield rather than John and Charles Wesley.

The Wesleys received their "new living faith" more than two years after Whitefield's preaching attracted many large crowds, beginning the English revival. Knowing they did not have the faith Whitefield had and preached, John and Charles began to seek faith, finally receiving their "full rebirth" by faith in Christ in May 1738.

The Wesleys and Whitefield were all members of the Holy Club at Oxford, founded and led by John Wesley. Therefore, the revival has been credited to him. A quick review of all their journals will clearly show it was Whitefield who led John and Charles into the open-air evangelism which saved England and recharged Christianity throughout the English-speaking world.

To correct the myths, George Whitefield must be acknowledged as the first evangelist of the revival that came to be known as Methodism. In addition, none of the Holy Club members ever intended a new Christian denomination to spring out of the revival. The movement was abhorred and widely criticized by the established state Church of England. Here, as in first-century Israel, God placed His Spirit and the gifts and fruit of that Spirit into the hands of common people with a religious heritage, then set them free from denominational hierarchy, polity, and dogmatics. This new band of English Christians sought only to find God's will and to please Him by following His will.

In 1736, God anointed George Whitefield with the gift of evangelism. His timing was perfect. The need for revival was immediate. Christian faith was nearly lost in England and its New World colonies. Man's cold-heartedness was the rule of the times. Living in this western end of European civilization had become, for most, a miserable, daily experience of poverty, hunger, sickness, and oppression.

The Jews in Egypt had had faith to seek deliverance through prayer, but not the English. Lacking both faith in God and understanding of their predicament, they sank into deep national alcoholism. Cheap gin, rampant prostitution, and human abuse were the lot of the average person. The wealthy, including some bishops, profited from the degradation. Just as in France and elsewhere on the Continent, monarchy had failed and was doomed to end in revolution unless God intervened.

From this morass, God selected a few ministerial students at prestigious Oxford University to start meeting together to grow in faith and improve their public expression of faith. These Holy Club members grasped the severity of the crisis but did not say so. Loyalty to the king was required of them as clergy of the Church of England. Their concern is evidenced by their efforts to bring relief to the needy, while, at the same time, seeking others to join them in their efforts.

Cynics found many epithets for the Holy Club and its members. One name finally stuck, being deemed properly insulting by the critics and flatteringly descriptive by its members. Those methodical doers of good works were called *Methodists*.

From 1738 to 1784, Methodism was the new spiritual leaven, bringing revival to both England and America. Through it, the power of the Holy Spirit was at work. The gifts and the fruit of the Spirit were manifest in the lives of its members and leaders.

In 1784, as a result of the American Revolution, American members of the movement broke all ties with the Church of England and created their new denomination, The Methodist Episcopal Church. Still later, in 1836, the English members of the movement broke from their state church and began ordaining their own ministers.

This book is not a step-by-step manual for starting a similar great revival. Rather, it is a composite of the journals of the three great leaders of Methodism along with a sample sermon from John Wesley. We will follow the revival through the eyes of its closest witnesses.

Hopefully, we will experience the flavor of revival, feel a quickening of our own spirits, and hunger for a repetition in our times. Hungering and thirsting for grace, along with asking, seeking, and knocking before God, provides the tinder and fuel that can again be ignited by the spark of His Holy Spirit.

Clare George Weakley, Jr.
Dallas, Texas, 1986

Part 1

The Human Messengers of Revival

1

John Wesley: From Works to Faith

As no other person can be so well acquainted with the revival (so-called Methodism) as I am, I feel obligated to leave, for the information of all, a clear account of the event. I do this because of the many published and unpublished charges of heresy placed against our revival and its leaders. George Whitefield, my brother Charles and I have written explanations of ourselves. Those published accounts, however, are too long to be quickly and easily read, so it seems useful to give serious inquirers a brief version of those events. Those desiring to have a fuller account of the revival may, at their leisure, read all of our journals.[1]

I believe till I was about ten years old I had not sinned away that washing of the Holy Ghost given me in baptism. I had been strictly and carefully taught that I could be saved only by complete obedience, by keeping all the commandments of God. Those instructions, so far as they respected outward duties and sins, I gladly received, and thought of often. But all that was said to me about inward obedience, or holiness, I neither un-

---

[1]John Wesley, *The Works of the Rev. John Wesley* (London: Wesleyan Conference Office, 1872), Volume XIII, p. 303, "A Short History of the People Called Methodists."

derstood nor remembered. So I was as ignorant of the true meaning of the law as I was of the gospel of Christ.

Outward Restraints Removed

The next six or seven years were spent at school. There, outward restraints being removed, I was much more negligent than before, even of outward duties. I was almost continually guilty of outward sins, and I knew it, though they were not scandalous in the eyes of the world. However, I still read the Scriptures and said my prayers morning and evening. I hoped to be saved by my own effort. This consisted of not being so bad as other people, having goodwill toward religion, reading the Bible, going to church, and saying my prayers.

While attending Oxford University for five years, I still said my prayers, both in public and in private. Also, I read, with the Scriptures, several other books of religion, especially commentaries on the New Testament. Yet I had not even a notion of inward holiness. Instead, I went on habitually, and for the most part very contentedly, in conscious sin. I had some intermission from sin and short struggles with it, especially before and after the holy communion, which I was required to receive three times a year. I cannot recall by what means I had hoped to be saved, while continually sinning against the little light I had— unless by those passing fits of what others taught me to call repentance.

A New Religious Friend

When I was about twenty-two, my father encouraged me to enter the ministry. At the same time, God directed me to read Kempis' *Christian's Pattern*. I began to see that true religion was seated in the heart, and that God's law extended to all our thoughts, not only words and actions. I was, however, angered at Kempis' strictness, yet, comforted in reading his work. Such comfort had been an utter stranger to me before. It was like meeting with a new religious friend.

I began to alter the whole form of my conversation and to move in earnest upon a new life. I set apart an hour or two a day for religious study and meditation. I took communion every week. I guarded against all sin, whether in word or deed. I began to aim at, and pray for, inward holiness. Now, doing so much and living such an exemplary life, I was sure I was a good Christian.

Changing to another college within the university, I made a resolution that I was convinced was of utmost importance. Shaking off at once all my trifling acquaintances, I began to see more clearly the value of time and applied myself closer to study. I guarded against actual sins and advised others to be religious, according to that scheme of religion by which I modeled my own life. I read William Law's *Christian Perfection* and *Serious Call.* Although I was offended by many parts of both books, they convinced me of the exceeding height, breadth and depth of the law of God. His light flowed mightily upon my soul, making everything appear in a new view. I cried to Him for help and resolved to obey Him. I purposed to keep His whole law, both inwardly and outwardly. By this would I be accepted by Him, and therefore saved.

Turning the War Against the World

While at Oxford, my brother and I and two more agreed to spend three or four evenings a week together. Our plan was to read over the classics on week nights, and on Sunday some book on theology. The following summer, William Morgan told me he had visited the jail to see a man who was condemned for killing his wife. From that and the talk he had with another of the prisoners, he believed it would be beneficial to speak with them occasionally. He repeated this so often that my brother and I finally accompanied him to the prison. We were well satisfied with the results and agreed to go back once or twice a week. Before long, he asked me to go with him to see a poor

woman nearby who was sick. This work, too, we believed would
be worthwhile. We planned to spend a couple of hours each week
in visitation, provided the minister of that particular parish
did not object.

In order not to depend wholly on our own judgments, I wrote
my father, a minister, of our plan, asking his advice as to
whether we had gone too far, and whether we should now stand
still, or go forward.

I received the following reply:

> As to your plans, I greatly approve. I have the highest rea-
> son to bless God that He has given me two sons together at
> Oxford. He has given you grace and courage to turn the war
> against the world and the devil, which is the best way to con-
> quer them. You have but one more enemy to combat—the flesh,
> which, if you take care to subdue by fasting and prayer, will
> set you free to proceed steadily in the same course and expect
> 'the crown which fadeth not away.'
>
> Go on, then, in God's name, in the path to which your Savior
> has directed you, and that track wherein your father has gone
> before you! For when I was an undergraduate at Oxford, I vis-
> ited those in the same prison, and reflect on it with great sat-
> isfaction to this day. Walk as prudently as you can, though not
> fearfully, and my heart and prayers are with you.

Persecuted for Righteousness' Sake

Soon after, one of our company, now five persons, told us
that he had been much abused the day before for being a member of "The Holy Club." It had become a common topic of mirth
at his college, where they accused us of customs which we did
not do.

When the outcry increased daily, we proposed to our opponents these and similar questions:

> Does it not concern all men of all conditions to imitate
> Jesus, who went about doing good? Are all Christians not con-
> cerned in that command, "While we have time let us do good
> to all men"? Shall we not be more happy hereafter, the more
> good we do now?

Can we be happy at all hereafter unless we have, according to our power, "fed the hungry, clothed the naked, visited those that are sick, and in prison"; and made all those actions subservient to a higher purpose, even the saving of souls from death?

Is it not our duty always to remember that He did more for us than we can do for Him, who assures us, "Inasmuch as ye have done it to one of the least of these my brethren, ye have done it unto me"?

On these considerations, may we not try to do good to our acquaintances? Particularly, may we not try to convince them of the necessity of being Christians? Is there a necessity of being scholars?

Is there a necessity of method and industry to order either learning or virtue?

May we not try to persuade them to confirm and increase their industry by communicating as often as they can? May we not mention to them the authors whom we conceive to have written the best on these subjects?

May we not assist them, as we are able from time to time, to form resolutions upon what they have read in those authors, and to execute them with steadiness and perseverance?

Also, upon the considerations above mentioned, may we not try to do good to those who are hungry, naked, or sick? In particular, if we know any needy family, may we not give them a little food, clothes, or medicine as they need?

May we not give them, if they can read, a Bible, Common-Prayer Book, or Whole Duty of Man?

May we not, now and then, inquire how they have used them, explain what they do not understand, and reinforce what they do?

May we not teach them the necessity of private prayer, and of frequenting the church and communion?

May we not contribute what little we are able toward having their children clothed and taught to read?

May we not take care that they are taught their catechism and short prayers for morning and evening?

Lastly, upon the considerations above, may we not try to do good to those who are in prison? In particular, may we not release well-disposed persons remaining in prison for whatever small payments they may owe?

May we not lend smaller sums to those who are of any trade, so they may procure tools and materials for work?

May we not give to those who appear to need it most a little money, or clothes, or medicine?

I do not remember meeting with any person who answered any of those questions in the negative. None ever doubted whether it was lawful to apply to this use the time and money we would have spent in other diversions. Several with whom we met increased our little stock of money for the prisoners and the poor by pledging something to it quarterly.

The Butt of Mirth and Anger

Almost as soon as we had made our first attempts this way, some of the cynics at college entered the ranks against us. Between mirth and anger, they made many reflections upon the "Sacramentarians," as they called us. Soon after, their allies changed our title and did us the honor of styling us "The Holy Club."

But most of them were persons of well-known bad character. They failed to gain any proselytes from the church till a gentleman, eminent for learning and well esteemed for piety, joined them. He told his nephew that if he dared to go to the weekly communion any longer, he would immediately cease his support. That argument, indeed, had no success; the young gentleman took communion that week. Then his uncle, having again tried to convince him that he was in the wrong by shaking him by the throat to no avail, changed his method. By mildness, he prevailed upon his nephew to absent himself from communion the following Sunday, as he did five Sundays out of six thereafter.

This much delighted our opponents, who rapidly increased in number. Shortly after, one of the seniors of the college sent for two young gentlemen, separately, who had taken communion weekly for some time. He was so successful in his exhortations that for the future they promised to take communion only three times a year. About this time there was a meeting of several of the officers and seniors of the college, wherein it was agreed upon what would be the speediest way to stop the progress of our enthusiasm.

It was soon publicly reported the censors were going to blow up "The Godly Club." That became our common title, though we were sometimes dignified with that of "The Enthusiasts," or "The Reforming Club." As for the names of Methodists, Supererogation-men, and so on, with which some of our neighbors were pleased to compliment us, we did not conceive ourselves to be under any obligation to consider them, much less to take them for arguments.

Diligently Striving Against Sin

So I began visiting the prisons and assisting the poor and sick in town. I did what good I could, by my presence or my little money, to the bodies and souls of all men. To this end I ridded myself of all luxuries, many which were necessities of life. I soon became known for this work, and I rejoiced that I was criticized for it.

The next spring I began observing the Wednesday and Friday fasts, commonly observed in my church, by eating no food till three in the afternoon. Now, I didn't know how to go any further. I diligently strove against all sin, omitting no sort of self-denial I thought useful. I carefully used, both in public and in private, all the means of grace at all opportunities. I omitted no occasion of doing good, and for that reason I suffered evil. All this I knew to be useless unless it was directed toward inward holiness. Accordingly, in all, I aimed at the image of God by doing His will, not my own. Yet after continuing some years in this way, I found myself near death. All my holiness brought me no comfort or assurance of acceptance with God. I was very surprised at this. I had been building on sand, never knowing that no other foundation can man lay than that which is laid by God, even Jesus Christ.

Soon after, a contemplative man convinced me still more that outward works alone are nothing. In several conversations he instructed me to pursue inward holiness, or a union of the soul with God. He recommended mental prayer as the most effectual means of purifying the soul, and uniting it with God. Initially I clung to his words as I did to God's, replacing my outward works with the pursuit of union with God. But now looking back, I had simply substituted one set of works for another. Pursuit of union with God was still my own righteousness just as visiting prisoners and the sick had been. In this refined way of trusting to my own works and my own righteousness, so zealously recommended by the mystic writers, I dragged on heavily, finding no comfort or help in it.

Too Educated and Too Wise

Later, on shipboard to America, I was again active in outward works. There it pleased God of His free mercy to give me twenty-six of the Moravian brethren for companions, who endeavored to show me "a more excellent way." But I could not understand it at first. I was too educated and too wise, so it seemed foolishness to me. I continued preaching, trusting in the righteousness of good works through which no one can be pardoned and saved.

All the time I was in America, I was just beating the air. Being ignorant of the righteousness of Christ, which, by a living faith in Him, brings salvation to everyone who believes, I continued seeking to establish my own righteousness. And so I continued laboring in the fire. I was now properly under the law. I knew the law of God was spiritual. I consented to it. I delighted in it after the inner man. Yet I was carnal and in sin. Every day I cried out, "For that which I do I allow not: for what I would, that do I not; but what I hate, that do I. . . . For to will is present with me; but how to perform that which is good I find not. For the good that I would I do not; but the evil which I would not, that I do. . . . I find then a law, that, when I would do good, evil is present with me. . . . But I see another law in my members, warring against the law of my mind, and bringing

me into captivity to the law of sin which is in my members"
(Rom. 7:15–23).

In this abject state of bondage to sin, I was continually fighting but not conquering. Before, I had willingly served sin. Now,
it was unwillingly, but still I served it. I fell, and rose, and fell
again. Sometimes I was overcome and in depression. Sometimes
I overcame and was in joy. As I had some of the foretastes of
the terrors of the law, so had I in this some of the comforts of
the gospel. During this whole struggle between nature and
grace, which had continued for about ten years, I had many
remarkable answers to prayer, especially when I was in trouble.
I had many comforts which are indeed no other than short
anticipations of the life of faith. But I was still under the law,
not under grace. Such is the state in which most who are called
Christians are content to live and die. I was only striving with,
not freed from, sin. I did not have the witness of the Spirit with
my spirit, and indeed could not, for I sought it not by faith but
by the works of the law.[2]

My thoughts on this were included in my journal entry upon
my return to England from America:

> I want that faith which none can have without knowing
> that he has it. Many imagine they have it who do not, for
> whoever has it is freed from sin, the whole body of sin is de-
> stroyed in him. He is freed from fear, having peace with God
> through Christ, and rejoicing in hope of the glory of God. And
> he is freed from doubt, having the love of God shed abroad in
> his heart through the Holy Ghost which is given him, the Spirit
> himself bearing witness with his spirit that he is a child of
> God.[3]

During my return to England, I was in imminent danger of
death, which made me very uneasy. I was strongly convicted
that the cause of my uneasiness was unbelief and that gaining
a true, living faith was the one thing I needed. Still, I did not

---

[2]Nehemiah Curnock, Ed., *John Wesley's Journal (Abridged)* (London: The Epworth Press, 1958 reprint), pp. 46–49, entry of May 24, 1738.
[3]*Ibid.*, p. 37, entry of February 1, 1738.

seek this faith as the right object. I sought faith only in God, not in or through Christ. Again, I did not know that I was wholly void of true faith. I only thought I did not have enough trust.

"It Was Clear I Had No Faith"

When I arrived in London, I met a Moravian by the name of Peter Böhler, whom I believe God had prepared for me. He affirmed a true faith in Christ and had two evident fruits: dominion over sin and a constant peace from a sense of forgiveness. I was quite amazed and saw this as a new gospel.

If this was true, it was clear I had no faith. But I was not willing to be convinced of this fact. Therefore I disputed with all my might and labored to prove that one might have faith without those fruits, especially where the sense of forgiveness was missing. For I had been taught to construe away all the scriptures relating to this, and to call all who believed otherwise Presbyterians. Besides, I thought, no one could, in the nature of things, have such a sense of forgiveness and not feel it. But I did not feel it. If, then, there was no faith without this sense of forgiveness, all my pretensions to faith fell at once.

When I met Peter Böhler again, he consented to center the dispute on the issue which I desired, namely Scripture and experience. I first consulted the Scriptures. But when I put aside the interpretations of men and simply considered the words of God, comparing them together, attempting to illustrate the obscure by the plainer passages, I found they all were against me. I was forced to retreat to my last hold, that experience would never agree with the literal interpretation of those scriptures. Nor could I believe it to be true until I found some living witnesses of that experience.

Peter replied he could show me witnesses any time—if I desired it, the next day. Accordingly, the next day he came again with three others, all testifying of their personal experience that a true, living faith in Christ is inseparable from a sense of pardon for all past, and freedom from all present, sins. They agreed that this faith is the free gift of God, which He would surely bestow upon every soul who earnestly and perseveringly sought it.

Renouncing My Own Works

I was now thoroughly convinced, and by the grace of God I resolved to seek it to the end. I absolutely renounced all dependence, in whole or in part, upon my own works or righteousness, on which from my youth I had really grounded my hope of salvation, though I did not know it. To the constant use of all the other means of grace, I added continual prayer for this very thing, justifying, saving faith, and a full reliance on the blood of Christ shed for me. I trusted in Him as my Christ, as my sole justification, sanctification and redemption.

Thus I continued to seek faith, though with strange indifference, dullness, coldness and unusually frequent lapses into sin until Wednesday, May 24. I think it was about five in the morning that I opened my Testament to these words: "Whereby are given unto us exceeding great and precious promises: that by these ye might be partakers of divine nature" (2 Pet. 1:4). Just as I left my room, I opened the Bible to these words: "Thou art not far from the kingdom of God" (Mark 12:34).

· In the afternoon I was asked to go to St. Paul's. The anthem was, "Out of the depths have I cried unto thee, O Lord. Lord, hear my voice: Let thine ears be attentive to the voice of my supplications. If thou, Lord, shouldest mark iniquities, O Lord, who shall stand? But *there is* forgiveness with thee, that thou mayest be feared. Let Israel hope in the Lord: for with the Lord *there is* mercy, and with him *is* plenteous redemption. And he shall redeem Israel from all his iniquities" (Ps. 130:1–4, 7–8).

"I Felt My Heart Strangely Warmed"

In the evening I went very unwillingly to a society in Aldersgate Street, where someone was reading Luther's preface to the Epistle to the Romans. About a quarter before nine, while he was describing the change which God works in the heart through faith in Christ, I felt my heart strangely warmed. I felt I did trust in Christ, Christ alone, for salvation, and an assurance was given me that He had taken away my sins, even mine, and saved me from the law of sin and death.

I began to pray with all my might for those who had despitefully used me and persecuted me. I then testified openly to all there what I now first felt in my heart. But it was not long before the enemy suggested, "This cannot be faith; for where is the joy?" Then I was taught that peace and victory over sin are essential to faith in the Captain of our salvation; but as far as the transports of joy usually attending the beginning of it, especially in those who have mourned deeply, God sometimes gives and sometimes withholds them, according to the counsels of His own will.

After my return home, I was buffeted with temptations, but cried out and they fled. They returned again and again. As often as I lifted my eyes He sent me help from His holy place. And herein I found the difference between this experience and my former state. I was striving and fighting with all my might under the law as well as under grace. But then I was sometimes, if not often, conquered. Now I was always the conqueror.[4]

---

[4]*Ibid.*, pp. 49–51.

2

Charles Wesley: At Peace with God*

While I was waiting to leave Georgia to return to England on Saturday, October 16, 1736, my illness increased despite all the doctors did for me. I began to seriously consider my condition and at my evening hour of retirement found some benefit from Pascal's prayer in sickness. The next day, while I was speaking on spiritual religion at Mr. Chichley's, his wife observed that my thinking was much like William Law's. I was glad and surprised to hear him mentioned. All I knew of religion was through him. I found she was well acquainted with his *Serious Call to a Devout Life* and had one of the two copies that are in New England. I borrowed the book and passed the evening reading it to the Williams family. His daughter and he seemed satisfied and affected. Many appointed days for embarkation had come and gone without our leaving, but this was certainly to be the last. Accordingly, Mr. Millar came very early to take me to the ship. I mentioned the book I had borrowed

*Thomas Jackson, Ed., *The Journal of the Rev. Charles Wesley, M.A.*, (London: 1849, reprinted Taylor, South Carolina: Methodist Reprint Society, 1977 and Grand Rapids: Baker Book House Company) V. 1, pp. 55–97, entries of October 18, 1736 through May 24, 1738.

from his sister, Mrs. Chichley, and read him the characters of Cognatus and Uranius. He liked them and promised he would carefully read the entire book. Breakfast and dinner passed, but there was no summons to go on board. Tuesday and Wednesday I grew worse and worse. On Thursday I was forced to stay in bed because of pain. A friend came and labored to dissuade me from the voyage, promising to deliver my letters and papers himself and excuse me from my promised return. Others joined him, but I put an end to their pleading by assuring them nothing less than death could hinder my embarking.

On Friday, all things being at last in readiness, the wind providentially changed. This gave me three more days to try medical experiments. During that time, I vomited, purged, bled, perspired and took laudanum, which entirely drained me of the little strength I had left.

After three days I waked surprisingly better, though not yet able to walk. Dr. Graves came from Charlestown to see me and gave me medicine and advice, which he left in writing. He would take no fee for either. I received the same generosity from my other doctors. A little later I was brought a summons to go abroad. Mr. Price drove me to the wharf, stopping on the way to see some of my new friends from whom I had received all the kindness in their power to show.

When we came to the wharf, the boat was not ready, so we were forced to wait half an hour in the cold, open air. Finally I was helped into the boat and covered up. In about two hours we reached the ship and I went on board. I lay down in the stateroom, less fatigued with the passage than I had expected.

I had a tolerable night, though stripped of the conveniences I so long enjoyed on shore. In the morning, I began the doctor's regimen and quickly reaped the benefits. Five leagues at sea in our voyage, the wind changed and forced us back. In the evening it was fair and by next day we were carried clear of all land.

Soon I began public prayers in the Great Cabin. We seldom had more than the passengers present. I did not yet have strength to read the lesson, nor attention for any harder study than Clarendon's *History of the Rebellion*. In the night I was much upset by colic.

Storm at Sea

We were only two days out when the captain warned me of a storm approaching. It came in the evening at eight. The storm rose higher and higher, even after I thought it must have come full strength. I did not sleep all night, being obliged by the return of my flu to rise continually. At last the long-wished-for morning came, but brought no abatement of the storm. The raging sea quickly washed away our sheep and half our hogs, and drowned most of our fowl. The ship had been newly caulked at Boston, not carefully it now appeared, for being deeply laden, the sea streamed in at the sides so heavily that four men had all they could do, by continual pumping, to keep her above water. I rose and lay down in shifts but could remain in no posture very long. In vain I strove to pray. I prayed for power to pray and for faith in Jesus Christ, continually repeating His name. Finally I felt the virtue of that name and knew that I now was under the cover of the Almighty.

Tasting God's Comfort

At about three in the afternoon, the storm was at its height. I endeavored to encourage other passengers who were in the utmost agony of fear. I prayed with them and for them till four. But the ship ultimately took on so much water that the captain, finding it impossible to save her from sinking, cut down the mizzen mast. In this dreadful moment, I found the comfort of hope and such a joy in finding a hope the world could neither give nor take away. I had a conviction of the power of God being with me, overruling my strongest passion and fear, raising me above what I am by nature and giving me a taste of His divine goodness.

At the same time, I found myself desiring in spirit to bear witness to the truth, perhaps for the last time, before my poor friend, Appee. I went to him and declared the difference between one who fears God and one who doesn't. I witnessed about my hope, not because I had attained it, but because I had endeavored for it. I testified of my expectation: if God should now require my soul, He would receive it to His mercy.

My friend was convinced but ignorant. He said his refuge in time of danger was to persuade himself that there was no danger. While others frequently called upon God to have mercy upon their souls, Appee confessed he greatly envied them, as he had no concern for his own. I advised him to pray. He answered that it was mocking God to begin praying when in danger if he had never done it when in safety. I added that I hoped if God spared him now, he would immediately begin working out his salvation, which depended on the one condition of exchanging this world for the next. Another passenger was present during this conversation and behaved as a Christian ought.

I returned to the other passengers and endeavored to show them that their fear reflected their lack of spiritual life, which was intended for our support on such occasions. I urged them to resolve, if God saved them from this distress, that they would instantly and entirely give themselves up to Him.

The wind was still as high as ever, but the motion was less violent since cutting the mast, keeping the ship from taking on so much water. I lay down utterly exhausted, but my sickness had so increased that I was unable to rest. Toward morning the sea heard and obeyed the divine voice, "Peace, be still!" (Mark 4:39).

Too Sick to Pray

On Sunday, my business was to offer up the sacrifice of praise and thanksgiving. Then we all joined in thanks for our deliverance. I was in bed most of the day, faint and full of pain. At night I rose for prayers but could not read them. I became so nauseated I vomited. This gave me immediate relief, and I passed the rest of the night in ease.

On the afternoon of the fifth day out, the wind rose, warning of another storm. I endeavored to prepare myself and my companions for the onslaught. The storm did not fail our expectation, but it was not so violent as the last. The sea broke over us every ten minutes. Between that and the ceaseless noise of the pumps, we were either prevented sleep or continually interrupted. After twenty-four hours, the poor sailors still had no respite, and as their strength drained, their murmurings increased. That night, when almost exhausted, they were relieved by a calm.

The following evening the wind and the sea arose again. At ten the sea broke in through one of the skylights and filled the Great Cabin. It was impossible to look for rest in such a hurricane. I waited until two in the morning for its abatement, but it continued all the following day in full strength.

"Throw the Cargo Overboard"

Nine days from embarkation, we met a ship bound for Boston, which had been ten weeks on her passage from Bristol. She was forced in the last storm to throw most of her cargo overboard. Being short of provisions, they asked for a barrel of beef. Our captain very readily sent them the food, though at the expense of much time and pains. He also sent a keg of rum to encourage their sailors to pump. The wind became fair about midnight, but soon returned to the same direction. Three days later, my flu returned violently.

After two weeks in voyage, the men came down and declared they could not keep the water out any longer. It was gaining upon them every moment. Therefore, they requested the captain to please lighten the ship. He told them he knew what he had to do and bade them return to their pumping, ordering others to take in all but the mainsail. He stayed some time, that he might not discourage us, and then went up. Taking in the sails helped considerably, though it still necessitated the constant effort of four men to keep the ship from filling.

During this time, I often threw myself upon the bed, seeking rest but finding none. I asked God to allow me a little rest so I might recover strength. Then I cast my eye upon the Scripture, "For my Name's sake will I defer mine anger, and for my praise will I refrain for thee, that I cut thee not off" (Isa. 48:9). My soul immediately returned to its rest, and I no longer felt the continuance of the storm.

Stopping the Leaks

Toward night of the next day, it pleased God to abate the wind, so that I once more enjoyed the comfort of sleep. After seventeen days of bad weather, on Saturday, November 13, never was a calm more needed than that which Providence sent us. The men were so harassed, they could work no longer. The leaks increased so fast that no less than their uninterrupted labor could have kept the vessel from foundering. All hands were now employed in stopping the leaks. The captain himself told us he had been extremely frightened the day before because of a danger he would now relate to us since it was over. There was total stoppage of one of the pumps. He further informed us that he had stopped several openings in the sides of the ship wide enough to lay his fingers in. He wondered how the poor men had been able to keep her above water. He added that the utmost he had hoped for was holding out till they could reach some of the western islands. Just as the men had finished their work, the calm gave place to a fair wind.

At midnight, Tuesday, November 23, I was awakened by a great uproar. So prodigious a sea broke upon the ship that it filled it and half-drowned the men on deck, though by a particular providence none were washed overboard. The swell lasted a little longer than the rain and high wind. In the morning we had our fair wind again, now twelve days since good winds first attended us.

In the afternoon we had another short but fierce blast, which brought the wind still fairer for our running into the Channel, which all agreed could not be far.

But our wind failed us. When it was first sent, we had not, in three weeks' sailing, reached the banks of Newfoundland, which was a third of our way. But this fortnight had almost brought us home. Toward evening on Saturday the weather became as fair as we could wish.

Land!

We were awakened between six and seven on Monday, November 29, by the captain crying out, "Land!" It was Lizard Point, about a league distant. What wind there was, it was for us. I felt thankful for His divine mercies.

The first thing I heard at daybreak on Wednesday, December 1, was the captain in an outrageous passion. The ship, which according to the course he had ordered, ought to have been near the coast of France, was, through the carelessness of the mate, just upon the land at Shoreham. He told me that had daylight not come when it did, the ship would have run aground. But in our lesser fate, all the art of man could not have saved her, for we were landlocked on three sides, with the wind right astern. It was with the utmost difficulty, and not until the afternoon, that we cleared. This lost us a day, for by the evening we should have reached the Downs.

On Thursday, by four in the afternoon, we came within sight of Beachy Head, but the wind freshened, and by nine we found ourselves almost unawares over against Dover. We fired a gun for a pilot, but none would come to us. We fell down into the Downs, over against Deal, and fired two more shots. The captain gave us notice that he expected a pilot in an hour or two at the most. I returned thanks to God for bringing us to the haven where we wanted to be and got my few things in readiness. Then I lay down, without disquiet or impatience, for two or three hours.

At six on Friday the pilot came on board. It was with much difficulty we got into his boat. The sea was so rough that nothing less than our late series of deliverances could have given us the confidence to try. In half an hour we reached the shore. I knelt down and blessed Him who had conducted me through such inextricable mazes, and asked that I might give up my country again to God when He should require that of me.

Alive from the Dead

I joined with the passengers in a hearty thanksgiving for our safe arrival. Then, between ten and eleven, we set out in the coach. By three we reached Canterbury, and by ten, Sittingbourne. At six in the evening of December 4, we arrived safe in London. I immediately took a coach for Charles Rivington's. My namesake rejoiced much at seeing me, and gave me great cause of rejoicing by his account of our Oxford friends.

My first Sunday home, I received comfort from communion at St. Paul's. From there I went to Mr. Towers, who received me with great affection and heartily congratulated me on my arrival, of which my friends had long despaired.

The next one I visited was Sir John Phillips, who received me as one alive from the dead. Here I heard a most blessed account of our friends at Oxford—their increase, both in zeal and number.

From my return on December 6, until the middle of the following January, my days were filled with visiting friends, clergy, and reporting to the Georgia Colony trustees. Too often, the recurring bouts with flu and continuing sickness interfered with my plans.

Then on Wednesday, January 19, the Moravian, Count Zinzendorf, arrived from Germany and sent for me. When I came, he saluted me with all possible affection and made me promise to come every day. I also visited the Bishop of Oxford, where I received an equally kind reception and was asked to come as often as I could. I accepted his open invitation and talked much with him, our conversation usually centering around the state of religion and of Count Zinzendorf's intended visit. During our time together, he affirmed his belief that Moravian bishops had the true succession. The following Saturday, January 22, I called on Mrs. Pendarvis. When I arrived she was reading a letter of my alleged death. Happy for me had the news been true. What a world of misery would it save me!

Free from that Moment

Two weeks passed before I had much conversation again with Count Zinzendorf. One of his beliefs was, "The Christian cannot yield to sin, cannot long fight against it, but must conquer it if he will." Speaking of his own case, he said he and a lady had been very much in love with each other. But feeling God's call so strongly on his life, he felt he should break the relationship and then persuaded her to marry a friend. "From that moment," said he, "I was freed from all self-seeking, so that for the past ten years I have not done my own will in anything, great or small. My own will is hell to me. I can now renounce my dearest friend without the least reluctance if God would require it." With the evident joy of the Lord, he kissed and blessed me as we parted. The following day, before I set out for Oxford, I called on the Count to ask for his prayers.

When I arrived at Oxford, I took up my lodgings with a Mr. Sarney. In the evening I met and encouraged our friends according to the Moravians' example. One friend, Charles Kinchin, I found changed into a courageous soldier of Christ. I also visited my old friends at the prison and found honest Thomas Waite still a prisoner there.

Toward the end of July I heard at Oxford that Charles Graves, a Holy Club brother, had been carried away by his friends, accused of being stark mad.

"Renounce Yourself!"

In August I began traveling by horseback, reading prayers and preaching. At Wormley, after giving communion to a sick woman, I had breakfast with Mr. Chadwick. We had some warm discussion about the new birth, with which he was greatly moved. I recommended that he have regular devotional times and seek out religious acquaintances.

Later, I visited at length about my spiritual state with William Law, at Putney. The sum of his advice was, "Renounce yourself and be not impatient."

In September I consulted Mr. Law a second time and asked him several questions.

"With what commentary shall I read the Scriptures?" I inquired.

"None," he replied.

"What do you think of one who dies unrenewed while endeavoring after it?" I asked further.

"It concerns neither you to ask, nor me to answer," was his reply.

"But shall I write once more to such a person?" I probed.

"No," was his flat answer.

"But I am persuaded it will do him good," I continued.

"Sir, I have told you my opinion," he affirmed strongly.

"Shall I write to you?" I queried.

"Nothing I can either speak or write will do you any good," he stated firmly.

Sunday, September 11, I preached on the one thing needed, the new birth. On Monday, I spent an hour in discoursing on the inward change, and reading William Law. Tuesday, I went again to my simple Hetty, to learn some of her humility. Her convictions were much deepened by my reading the *Life of God in the Soul of Man.* I took my leave, and set out for Oxford, by way of Windsor and Mr. Thorold's.

In a few days, I rose with an earnest desire to die to self entirely. From September into October, I traveled much on horseback to preaching appointments. Visiting with friends, I was able to preach on the one thing needed, Christ.

Not with Persuasive Words of Wisdom . . .

During this time, I heard George Whitefield preach on several occasions, including October 30 at Forster Lane and College Street. On Saturday, November 5, I returned to hear George Whitefield preach again. He preached not with the persuasive words of man's wisdom, but with the demonstration of the Spirit and with power. The churches could not contain the multitudes that thronged to hear him.

Sunday, November 13, I spoke at Bexley, on the love of God. One person, Mrs. Delamotte, with tears in her eyes, thanked me for my sermon. Later, we conversed some more on the love of God. This time Mr. Delamotte confessed that there could be no happiness in anything else. Little Molly burst into tears upon my telling her God loved her. The whole family now appear not far from the Kingdom of God.

At St. Helen's, November 20, I preached on the circumcision of the heart. The next day I became ill with the flu again.

In February, 1738, my brother John, returned from Georgia and we resumed our work at Oxford. Late that month, I began meeting with Peter Böhler. On Wednesday, February 22, at five, I had some earnest conversation with Peter, who pressed upon our scholars the necessity of prayer and faith.

Sickness unto Death

On Friday, February 24, at six in the evening, I suffered a severe toothache. I smoked tobacco, which made me nauseated and I was unable to keep anything down, taking away both my senses and pain. At eleven I awakened in extreme pain, which I thought would quickly separate soul and body. Soon after, Peter Böhler came to my bedside and I asked him to pray for me. He seemed unwilling at first, but, beginning very faintly, he raised his voice by degrees and prayed for my recovery with strange confidence. Then he took me by the hand and calmly said, "You will not die now." I thought within myself, *I cannot hold out in this pain till morning. If it abates before, I believe I may recover.*

He asked me, "Do you hope to be saved?"

"Yes," I replied.

"For what reason do you hope to be saved?" he pressed.

"Because I have used my best endeavors to serve God," I assured him.

He shook his head and said no more. I thought him very uncharitable, saying in my heart, *"What! Are not my endeavors sufficient ground for hope? Would he rob me of my endeavors? I have nothing else to trust to.*

By morning the pain had moderated somewhat. One of my friends, Ted Bentham, called and persuaded me to be bled. I continued in great pain throughout the day. In the evening Bentham brought Dr. Manaton and he performed the procedure. On Saturday morning the treatment was repeated again, and at night a third time. On Monday the scale seemed to turn for life. I had prayed that my pains might not outlast this day and my prayer was answered. Through March I recovered slowly from my illnesses, which, some say, brought me near the jaws of death.

Instantaneous Conversion

On April 20, while in London, I had the satisfaction of once more meeting that man of God, Peter Böhler. A few days later at a meeting in our little chapel, we sang and later fell into a dispute whether conversion was gradual or instantaneous. My brother John was very positive for the latter. Very shockingly he mentioned some late instances of gross sinners believing in a moment. I was much offended at his, I thought, worse-than-unedifying discourse. A lady left the meeting abruptly, but I stayed and insisted a man need not know when first he had faith. John's obstinacy in favoring the contrary opinion at last drove me out of the room. After dinner my brother returned to town. I stayed behind and read the *Life of Mr. Halyburton.* I could find only one instance of instantaneous conversion. I returned to London on Friday, April 28. No sooner had I arrived at James Hutton's, having moved my things there from his father's place, than the pain in my side returned, accompanied by a high fever. Toward midnight I received some relief by bleeding, performed by Dr. Cockburn. In the morning the doctor came to see me, as well as a better physician, Peter Böhler, whom God had detained in England for my good. Peter stood by my bedside and prayed that I might now see the divine intention in his being detained and my being ill. I immediately thought it might be that I should again consider Böhler's doctrine of faith, examine myself whether I was in the faith; and if I was not, never cease seeking and longing until I attained it.

No Peace Without Forgiveness

The following Monday, Mr. Piers came to see me. I exhorted him to seek that faith which he thought I had and I knew I didn't. After receiving communion, I felt a small anticipation of peace, and said, "Now I have a demonstration against the Moravian doctrine, that a man cannot have peace without assurance of his pardon. I now have peace, yet cannot say of a surety that my sins are forgiven." The next few times I took communion, I received no peace. God no longer trusted me with a comfort that I could immediately turn against Him.

For some days following I felt a faint longing for faith and could pray for nothing else. My desires were quickened by a letter of Mr. Edmunds', seeking Christ as if in agony. When Saturday, May 6, came, God still nurtured the little spark of desire which He himself had kindled in me. I seemed determined to speak of and wish for nothing but faith in Christ. Yet this could not preserve me from sin, which this day I saw with my eyes open. After ten years' vain struggling, I owned and felt sin to be absolutely unconquerable. By bearing witness to this truth before others, I found my desires of apprehending Christ increased.

To the House of a Godly Man

On Thursday, May 11, as I was just about to move to John Hutton's, God sent John Bray to me. He is a poor, ignorant mechanic who knows nothing but Christ, yet by knowing Him, knows and discerns all things. Some time ago I had left Peter Böhler, confessed my unbelief and lack of forgiveness, but declared firm persuasion that I should receive the atonement before I died. His answer was, "According to your faith be it unto you" (Matt. 9:29).

John Bray now replaced Böhler's place in my life. We prayed together for faith. I was quite overcome and melted into tears, and, by that, induced to think it was God's will that I should go to his house and not elsewhere. Bray was of the same persuasion. Accordingly, too ill to walk, I was carried there in a chair.

I found John's sister in earnest pursuit of Christ, and his wife well inclined to conversion. John Bray read many encouraging scriptures to me, which greatly strengthened my desire for faith. I was determined not to leave his house before I believed with my heart unto righteousness and received the faith I sought.

The next day I awakened in the same blessed state of mind—hungry and thirsty after God. I began reading Isaiah and seemed to see that the promises were made to me and would be fulfilled, for Christ loved me. I found myself more desirous, more assured, that I could believe. This day, and indeed my whole time, I spent in discoursing on faith, whether with those who had it or those who sought it, and in reading the Scripture and in prayer. Joining with John Bray in prayer and the Scripture, I was so greatly affected that I almost thought Christ was coming that moment. I concluded the night with private, vehement prayer.

Longing to Find Christ

On Saturday, May 13, I awakened without Christ, yet still desiring to find Him. William Delamotte came and read Psalm 68 to me, a psalm strangely full of encouraging promises. Toward noon I was able to pray with desire and hope, and to lay claim to the promises in general. I spent the afternoon with my friends in mutual exhortation to wait patiently for the Lord in prayer and reading. At night my brother John came. He was exceedingly heavy. I forced him, as he had often forced me, to sing a hymn to Christ, and almost thought Jesus would come while we were singing, being assured He would come quickly. At night I received much light and comfort from the Scriptures.

The beginning of Sunday, May 14, found me very heavy, weary, and unable to pray, but the desire soon returned and I found much comfort both in prayer and in the Word, my eyes being opened more and more to discern and lay hold on the promises. I longed to find Christ that I might show Him to all mankind, that I might praise, that I might love Him.

Another Gospel

Tuesday, I awakened weary, faint, and heartless. In the afternoon I seemed deeply aware of my misery in being without Christ. On Wednesday I experienced the power of Christ rescuing me in temptation. Today, Thursday, I first read Luther's writings on Galatians. I found Luther to be nobly full of faith. A friend, in hearing him, was so affected as to breathe out unutterable sighs and groans. I marveled that we could so soon and so entirely be removed from Him, who called us into the grace of Christ, unto any other gospel.

Who would believe our church had been founded on this important article of justification by faith alone? I am astonished

I should ever think this a new doctrine, especially while our doctrines stand unrepealed and the key of knowledge has not been taken away.

From this time forward, as many as came to visit me I endeavored to ground in this fundamental truth, *salvation by faith alone.* This is not an idle, dead faith, but a faith which works by love, and necessarily produces good works and all holiness.

I spent some hours in the evening in private with Martin Luther's writings on Salvation. He greatly blessed me, especially his conclusion of the second chapter. I labored, waited, and prayed to feel Him who loved me and gave himself for me. When exhaustion forced me to bed, I opened the book to these words: "For He will finish the work, and cut it short in righteousness, because a short work will the Lord make upon earth." After this assurance that He would come and would not tarry, I slept in peace.

About midnight on the 18th, I was awakened by the return of pleurisy. I felt great pain constricting my heart, but found immediate relief by being bled by a doctor. I thought myself willing to die the next moment, if I might die and believe, but was sure I could not die till I did believe. I earnestly desired it.

A Christless Communion

At five the morning of Friday, May 19, the pain and difficulty in breathing returned. The surgeon was sent for, but I fell asleep before he could bleed me a second time. Upon awakening, I received communion, but not Christ.

At seven, Mrs. Turner, Bray's sister, came and told me I should not rise from that bed till I believed. I believed her and asked, "Has God then bestowed faith on you?"

"Yes, He has," she answered.

"Why, have you peace with God?" I inquired.

"Yes, perfect peace," she answered.

"And do you love Christ above all things?" was my next question.

"I do—above all things incomparably," was her answer.
"Then you are willing to die?" I queried.

"I am," she said, "and would be glad to die this moment, for I know all my sins are blotted out. The handwriting that was against me is removed and nailed to His cross. He has saved me by His death. He has washed me with His blood. He has hidden me in His wounds. I have peace in Him and rejoice with joy unspeakable, full of glory."

Her answers so fully answered these and the most searching questions I could ask that I had no doubt of her having received the atonement. I waited for it myself with a more assured hope. Feeling an anticipation of joy upon hearing her account and thanking Christ as I could, I looked for Him all night with prayers and unceasing desires.

Failing Faith

Saturday, May 20, I awakened very disappointed and continued all day in great dejection. My communion with God did not change in the least. Nevertheless, God would not suffer me to doubt the truth of His promises. John Bray, too, seemed troubled at my not yet believing, and complained of his uneasiness and lack of patience.

"With me," he said, "when my faith begins to fail, God gives me some sign to support it."

He then opened a Testament and read the first words that he saw. "And he entered into a ship, and passed over, and came into his own city. And, behold, they brought to him a man sick of the palsy, lying on a bed: and Jesus seeing their faith said unto the sick of the palsy; Son, be of good cheer; thy sins be forgiven thee. And, behold, certain of the scribes said within themselves, This man blasphemeth. And Jesus knowing their thoughts said, Wherefore think ye evil in your hearts? For whether is easier, to say, Thy sins be forgiven thee; or to say, Arise, and walk? But that ye may know that the Son of man hath power on earth to forgive sins, (then saith he to the sick of the palsy,) Arise, take up thy bed, and go unto thine house. And he arose, and departed to his house. But when the multitudes saw it, they marvelled, and glorified God, which had given such power unto men" (Matt. 9:1-8).

It was a long while before he could read this through, for he was crying tears of joy. I saw in this, and firmly believed, that his faith would be available for my healing.

Pentecost Sunday, May 21, 1738, I awakened in hope and expectation of His coming. At nine my brother and some friends came and sang a hymn to the Holy Spirit. My comfort and hope increased. In about half an hour, they left and I began to pray. The substance was as follows: "Oh, Jesus, you have said, 'I will come to you.' You have said, 'I will send him, the Comforter, unto you.' You have said 'My Father and I will come unto you and make our abode with you.' You are God, who cannot lie. I wholly rely upon your most true promise. Accomplish this in your time and manner."

Faith Restored

Having prayed thus, I was relaxing for sleep, in quietness and peace, when I heard someone (Mrs. Musgrove, I thought) come in and say, "In the name of Jesus of Nazareth, arise, believe, and thou shalt be healed of all thy infirmities!"

I wondered how it should enter her head to speak in that manner. The words struck me to the heart. I sighed and said to myself, *Oh, that Christ would but speak thus to me.* I lay musing and trembling. Then I thought, *But what if it should be He? I will at least send for Mrs. Musgrove to see.*

I rang and Mrs. Turner came. I asked her to send Mrs. Musgrove to me. She went downstairs and, returning, said, "Mrs. Musgrove has not been here."

My heart sank within me at the words. I hoped it might be Christ indeed. However, I sent her down again to inquire. I felt in the meantime a strange palpitation of heart. I said, yet feared to say, *"I believe, I believe!"*

Mrs. Turner came up again and said, "It was I, a weak sinful creature, who spoke, but the words were Christ's. He commanded me to say them and so inspired me that I could not forbear."

I sent for John Bray and asked him whether I believed. He answered that I ought not to doubt it. It was Christ who spoke to me. He knew it and wanted us to pray together.

"But first," he said, "I will read what I have casually opened upon. Here it is, Psalm 32: 'Blessed is he whose transgression is forgiven, and whose sin is covered. Blessed is the man unto whom the Lord imputeth not iniquity, and in whose spirit there is no guile.' "

I still felt a violent opposition to believe. But yet the Spirit of God strove with both my own spirit and the evil spirit, until by degrees He chased away the darkness of my unbelief. I found myself convinced—I knew not how nor when—and immediately fell to intercession.

"Out of the Mouth of Babes"

Bray then told me his sister had been ordered by Christ to come and say those words to me—which she had earlier reported to me. She later related to me more at large the manner of her believing. At night, and nearly the moment I was taken ill, she dreamed she heard someone knock at the door. She went down and opened it and saw a person in white. She caught hold of him and asked who he was. "I am Jesus Christ," He had said, and she cried out with great vehemence, "Come in, come in!"

She awakened in a fright. It was immediately suggested to her that she must not mind this; it was only a dream. She continued feeling uneasy all day Friday till evening prayers. No sooner had they begun than she found herself so full of faith that she could scarce contain herself. She almost doubted whether she was sober. At the same time she was enlarged in love and prayer for all mankind, and commanded to go and assure me from Christ of my recovery—soul and body. She returned home repeating with all joy and triumph, "I believe, I believe." Yet her heart failed her, and she dared not say the words to me that night.

On Sunday morning she took her brother aside, burst into tears and informed him of the matter, protesting she was a poor, weak, sinful creature. Should she go to a minister? She could neither do it nor rest until she did. He asked whether she had ever found herself so before.

"No, never," she replied.

"Why, then," he said, "go. Remember Jonah. You declare promises, not threatenings. Go in the name of the Lord. Fear not your own weakness. You speak the words. Christ will do the work. 'Out of the mouth of babes and sucklings hast thou ordained strength,' God's Word says."

They prayed together and she then went up, but dared not come in until she had prayed again by herself. About six minutes after she had left him, her brother felt that Christ was with us while she was speaking the words. I had never heard words uttered with such solemnity. The sound of her voice was entirely changed into that of another person.

The Shield of Faith

I rose and looked into the Scripture. The words that I first saw were: "And now, Lord, what wait I for? My hope is in thee (Ps. 39:7). I then moved my eyes and met, "He hath put a new song in my mouth, even praise unto our God: many shall see it, and fear, and shall trust in the Lord" (Ps. 40:3,4). Afterward I opened to Isa. 40:1: "Comfort ye, comfort ye my people, saith your God. Speak ye comfortably to Jerusalem, and cry unto her, that her warfare is accomplished, that her iniquity is pardoned: for she hath received of the Lord's hand double for all her sins."

I now found myself at peace with God, and rejoiced in the hope of loving Christ. For the rest of the day, I mistrusted my own weakness—great, but now unknown. I saw that by the continual support of faith, I could stand, though of myself I would ever sink into sin. I went to bed still aware of my own weakness, yet confident of Christ's protection.

Under His protection I awakened the next morning and rejoiced in reading Psalm 107. It so nobly described what God had done for my soul. I fell asleep again and awakened out of a dream that I was fighting with two devils. I had one under my feet while the other at times faced me, then faded and vanished away upon my telling him I belonged to Christ.

More of His Strength

Now as the morning progressed, I saw Christ chiefly as my King, and found Him in His power. But I saw little of the love of Christ crucified, or of my past sins. I humbly hope that I saw more of my own weakness in view of His great strength. Many evil thoughts darted into my mind, but I rejected them all immediately. At noon I rose, continually fainting but nevertheless upheld. I was greatly strengthened by Isaiah 43, which God directed me to:

> But now thus saith the Lord that created thee, O Jacob, and he that formed thee, O Israel, Fear not: for I have redeemed thee, I have called thee by thy name; thou art mine. When thou passest through the waters, I will be with thee; and through the rivers, they shall not overflow thee: when thou walkest through the fire, thou shalt not be burned; neither shall the flame kindle upon thee. For I am the Lord thy God, the Holy One of Israel, thy Savior.

My brother was coming, so we joined in intercession for him. In the midst of prayer I almost believed the Holy Spirit was coming upon him. In the evening we sang and prayed again. I found myself very weak in body, but thought I ought to pray for my friends, being the only priest among them. I kneeled down and was immediately strengthened, both in mind and body. The enemy did not lose such an opportunity to tempt me to pride. But, God be praised, I ascribed my strength unto Him.

The Madness of Simple Faith

An old friend called to see me, fearing I was going mad. His fears were increased by my telling him that the prayer of faith had healed me when I was sick at Oxford. He expected to see the rays of light about my head, he said. I begged him, for his own sake, not to pass sentence until he had all the evidence concerning me. He could not promise this, but faintly prayed me to flee from London. In despair of me, he left.

It was morning before I could get to sleep. Many notions of pride arose, and were continually beaten down by Christ my King. The devil also tempted me to impatience through pain, but God turned it into an occasion of resignation.

The Battleground of the Heart

Tuesday, May 23, I awakened under the protection of Christ, and gave myself up, soul and body, to Him. At nine, I began a hymn about my conversion, but was persuaded to stop for fear of pride. John Bray came and encouraged me to proceed in spite of Satan's onslaught. I asked Christ to stand by me and there finished the hymn. Upon showing it to John afterwards, the devil threw me a fiery dart, suggesting that it was wrong and I had displeased God. My heart sank within me. Then casting my eye on a prayer book, I met with an answer for him, "Why boastest thou thyself, thou tyrant, that thou canst do mischief?" Upon this, I clearly discerned that the enemy's taunting was a device to keep me from giving glory to God. The devil will usually preach humility when speaking will endanger his kingdom or do honor to Christ. He would least like us to tell what things God has done for our souls, so pretentiously does he guard us from pride. But God has shown that He can defend me from pride while I'm speaking for Him.

Throughout this day I was kept in a constant sense of my own weakness. At night I was tempted to think the reason for my believing was my own sincerity. I rejected that thought with horror, and remained more than a conqueror through Him that loved me.

The following Wednesday, I was assaulted by the fear of my old accustomed deadness. I soon recovered confidence in Christ that He would give me as much sense of His love now as He saw good for me. I received communion without any feeling of devotion, only that I was afterward perfectly calm and satisfied, without doubt, fear, or scruple. We passed the afternoon in prayer, singing, and conversation.

John Believes!

At eight I prayed by myself for love, with some assurance of feeling more love. Toward ten, my brother was brought in triumph by a troop of our friends, and declared, "I believe!" We sang the hymn with great joy, then parted with prayer.

At midnight I committed myself to Christ, assured I was safe—sleeping or waking. I had continual experience of His power to overrule all temptation. I confessed with joy and surprise that He was able to do exceeding abundantly for me, above what I could ask or think.

3

*George Whitefield: Divine Employment**

"Come and hear, all ye who fear God, and I will declare what he has done for my soul" (Ps. 66:16).

Trinity Sunday, 1736, I was ordained at Gloucester, where I had been baptized. It was here that I preached my sermon "The Necessity and Benefit of Religious Society" to a very crowded congregation. I left the next Wednesday for Oxford, where I was received with great joy by my religious friends. For about a week I continued in my servitor's habit, and then took my degree of Bachelor of Arts. I had been at the university three and three-quarters years and was nearly twenty-two years old. My friends, John and Charles Wesley, were in Georgia. Since one or two more Holy Club members had taken churches, the interest in "Methodism," as it was then and is now termed, had visibly declined. Very few of this so-called "mad way" were left at the university. This somewhat discouraged me. But the Lord Jesus supported my soul and gave me a strong conviction that I was where He would have me.

---

*George Whitefield, *A Further Account of God's Dealings with George Whitefield*, (London: 1756 reprinted as *Journals of George Whitefield*, Grand Rapids: Christian Classics) pp. 37–50, June 1736–December 1737.

My degree gave me access to those I could not mix with in a lesser position. As opportunity offered, I was able to converse with them about the Kingdom of God.

During this time I was given charge over the donations for the poor prisoners, which amounted to about forty pounds per annum. Two or three small charity schools, maintained by the Methodists, were also under my immediate care. This, with the time I spent in following my studies, private devotions, and religious conversation, filled up my whole day.

I enjoyed distributing money and books among the poor prisoners and employing as many as could work. By this they were kept from that worst of jail diseases—idleness. They were not only convinced that we bore goodwill toward them, but were under obligation to hear the instructions we gave them from time to time. This program was first taken up by the Wesleys. I wish all Ordinaries* of prisons would copy their good example. They would deserve rewards from government and, if motivated by the love of God, would receive more glorious rewards from Him who said, "I was sick and ye visited me: I was in prison, and ye came unto me" (Matt. 25:36).

"Let No Man Despise Thy Youth!"

I soon became more than content in my state of life. I thought of staying at the university, at least for some years, to finish my studies and do what good I could among the despised poor. But God's thoughts are not man's thoughts; neither are His ways our ways. By a series of unexpected and unsought-for providences, I was soon called from my ease to journey to London. While an undergraduate, I became friends with Thomas Broughton, a confessed Methodist. He had recently been ordained and was now curate at the Tower of London. I frequently corresponded with him. When together, we exhorted each other

---

*A clergyman appointed formerly in England to give spiritual assistance to condemned criminals and to prepare them for the ordeal of the death penalty.

and walked to the house of God as friends.

Being called to Hampshire for a while, he wrote, encouraging me in my Christian walk and asking that I officiate in his absence. There, he said, I would be refreshed by many who loved me for Christ's sake and had for a long time desired to see me.

On Wednesday, August 4, with fear and trembling, I obeyed the summons and went by coach to London. I spent a good part of the way in earnest supplication to the God of all grace to be my guide and my comforter. At the same time I could not help praising Him for changing my heart. He had called me to preach at a place in which, not many years before, I would have given a great deal of money to see a play. That evening I reached the Tower and was kindly received by my friend. The remainder of the week was spent in visiting John Philips and others who were glad to see me.

But God sent me something to balance the joy of the task. As I passed along the streets, many came out of their shops to see a person so young in clerical garb. One, I remember in particular, cried out, "There's a boy parson!" I was mortified and prayed Paul's exhortation, "Let no man despise thy youth" (1 Tim. 4:12).

On Sunday afternoon, August 8, I preached at Bishopsgate Church. The largeness of both the church and the congregation at first dazed me a little. But looking to God and considering in whose name I was about to speak, my mind calmed and I was enabled to preach with power. The effect was immediate and visible to all. As I entered the pulpit, nearly everyone seemed to sneer at me because of my youth. But the congregation soon grew serious and exceedingly attentive. After I came down, they showed me great respect, blessing me as I passed along and asking others who I was. No one could answer that question, for I was a stranger. I slipped speedily through the crowd and returned to the Tower, blessing God for His goodness to me, the unworthiest of men.

I stayed there for two months, reading prayers twice a week, catechizing and preaching once, and visiting the soldiers in the infirmary and barracks daily. I also read prayers every evening at Wapping Chapel, and preached at Ludgate Prison every Tuesday. God gave me favor in the eyes of the inhabitants of the Tower. The chapel was crowded on the Lord's day. Many religious friends from various parts of town came to hear the Word. Several serious young men also came to hear me preach and teach about the new birth and the necessity of renouncing all in order to follow Jesus Christ.

An Irresistible Call

After I had been in town about a month, I received letters from the Wesleys in Georgia, and Benjamin Ingham, a fellow laborer. Their accounts fired my soul and made me long to go abroad for God, too. But having no outward call, and being too feeble, as I then thought, to ever undertake a voyage at sea, I tried to lay aside all thoughts of going abroad. But I could not. At times I felt such a strong attraction in my soul toward Georgia that I thought it almost irresistible. I strove against it with tears, praying that the Lord would not allow me to be deluded. At length I discussed my feelings with several friends. All agreed that laborers were wanted at home, that I had no visible call abroad, and that it was my duty not to be rash but to wait and see what Providence might point out to me. I consented to this with my whole heart.

Having stayed in London till Thomas Broughton came back from the country, I returned to my little charge at Oxford. There I waited upon my deaconship according to the measure of grace imparted to me.

Sweet Communion

I led a delightful life there, enjoying daily communion with God! My private hours glided away in reading and praying over Henry's *Comment upon the Scriptures*. (While I am writing about it, the fire I then felt again kindles in my soul.) Not only was I happy, but several other youths were also greatly quickened. We met daily in my room to encourage each other in the faith.

God also raised up friends for our financial support. The elect lady, Betty Hastings, was one of them. Another was a man whose heart was knit in a special manner to mine when I was at London. Without being solicited, he sent not only money for the poor, but also funds to pay debts I had incurred for books before I received my degree. Upon his recommendation I was chosen a member of the Society for Promoting Christian Knowledge. I rejoiced in this, as it gave me an opportunity to procure books cheaply for the poor people. May God continue to bless that society to the advancement of His own glory and His people's eternal good.

A Proud Heart

About the middle of November 1736, I was once more called from my little scene of action. Charles Kinchin, a minister of Dummer, had lately been awakened and resolved to associate with the despised Methodists, determining to know nothing but Jesus Christ and Him crucified. Being likely to be chosen Dean of Corpus Christi College, he asked me to come and officiate for him till that appointment was decided. I consented, and he served my place at Oxford.

Dummer consisted chiefly of poor and illiterate people. At first my proud heart could not take it. I would have given all the world for one of my Oxford friends, and mourned for lack of them as a dove that has lost her mate. Giving myself to prayer and reading William Law's story of Ouranious in his *Serious Call to a Devout Life* reconciled me to my place.

I generally divided the day into three parts: eight hours for study and retirement, eight hours for sleep and meals, and eight hours for reading prayers, catechizing, and visiting the parish. The profit I reaped by these exercises and by conversing with the poor country people was unspeakable. I frequently learned as much from an afternoon's visit as from a week's study. During my stay there, an invitation was sent me to take a very profitable ministry in London, but I had no inclination to accept it.

Resolving to Sail to Georgia

The thoughts of going to Georgia still continually crowded in upon me, and providence seemed to point in that direction. At length I resolved to embark for Georgia. Knowing that I would never put my resolution into practice if I conferred with others, I wrote to my relatives to inform them of my plans and told them that if they would promise not to dissuade me from my intended voyage, I would come and visit them. Otherwise, knowing my own weakness, I was determined to embark without visiting them at all.

On New Year's Day 1737, I went to Gloucester to seek my bishop's opinion and to visit my mother and other relatives. The bishop, as he always did, received me like a father. He approved my plan, wished me much success, and said he did not doubt but that God would bless me and I would do much good abroad. But my own family, at first, was not so passive. My aged mother wept much. Others reminded me what preferential treasure I might have if I would stay at home. However, finding my mind so fixed, they soon spoke against it no longer.

During my stay in Gloucester, God gave me honor for a while, even in my own country! I preached twice on the Sabbaths. Congregations were very large and the power of God attended the Word. I have reason to believe some were truly converted. They will be my joy and crown of rejoicing in the day of the Lord Jesus.

"Who Is This Man?"

In about three weeks I went to Bristol. It was my practice wherever I went, to attend the daily public offices of the church.

So I went the next Thursday to hear a sermon at St. John's Church. After prayers, while the Psalm was being sung, a minister came to me and asked if I would give the sermon. Having my notes with me, I complied. The people seemed startled, and after the sermon asked who I was. The next day there was another lecture at St. Stephen's. Many crowded in, expecting to hear me again.

The lecturer asked me to preach as the other had the day before. I again complied. The report given here was so generally good that on the following Lord's Day, many from all denominations crowded the churches where I preached. Afterward I was called by the mayor to preach before him and his officials. For some time following, I preached all the lectures on weekdays and twice on Sundays, besides visiting the religious societies.

Arrows of Conviction

The Word, through the mighty power of God, was sharper than a two-edged sword. The doctrine of the new birth and justification by faith in Jesus Christ made its way like lightning into the hearers' consciences, and the arrows of conviction stuck fast. My whole time between one lecture and another, except what was spent in necessary refreshment, was wholly occupied in talking with people about spiritual concerns. I received large offers to stay in Bristol. All wondered why I wanted to go to Georgia when I might be so well provided for at home. Some urged that if I wished to convert Indians, I might go to the Kingswood coal miners and find Indians enough there.

None of these things moved me. Having put my hand to the plough, I was determined through grace not to look back. Therefore, at length, I took my leave, but with mutual affection and concern that cannot easily be expressed.

In the middle of February, Lent was at hand. I was required to be at Oxford for the remainder of my college exercise, which they call "determining." On my way I went through Gloucester and stayed there a week, visiting the prisoners and encouraging the awakened souls.

Voyage Delayed

Having stayed about ten days, I came up to London in the beginning of March and continued there about three weeks, waiting and expecting to sail any day. I preached more frequently than when I was there before. Many more came to hear me, and the last Sunday I was in town, I read prayers twice and preached four times. But, finding the ship was not likely to go for some time, and being under obligation to Sampson Harris, minister of Stonehouse in Gloucestershire, I went at his request to replace him while he came up to dispatch some affairs in town.

I felt God had sent me to Gloucestershire in answer to prayer, for I learned of a little society of seeking souls who had heard me preach in an adjacent town. I wrestled with God to send me to them if it was His will. God confirmed my desire and I went. The people received me with joy, and I found them more knowing than I expected.

Having use of the parsonage, I expounded every night. Many who were not parishioners came to hear and were edified. On Sundays, besides teaching the lessons, catechizing, and preaching, I repeated my sermons to the society. Neither church nor house could contain the people that came.

An Unforgettable Night

I found uncommon manifestations granted me from God. Early in the morning, at noon, evening, and midnight the blessed Jesus visited and refreshed my heart. If the trees of a certain wood near Stonehouse could speak, they would tell what wonderful communion some others and I enjoyed with our blessed God there. Sometimes, as I was walking, my soul would make such leaps that it would almost go out of the body. At other times, I would be so overpowered with a sense of God's infinite majesty that I would throw myself on the ground and offer my soul to His hands to write on it what he pleased. One night especially was unforgettable. I had been expounding to many people, and some were afraid to go home. I thought it my duty to accompany them and to stir them up to prepare for the coming of Christ. Returning to the parsonage, I and a poor but pious countryman went to the field, exulting in our God and longing for that time when Jesus would be revealed from heaven in a flame of fire. *Oh, that my soul may be in a like frame when he will actually come to call me!* I think I never had been happier than that night or more blessed than during my time at Stonehouse.

Final Farewells

Every week the congregations increased. At the end of my stay, on Ascension Day, their sighs and tears almost broke my heart as I bade them farewell. Many cried out like Ruth, "Whither thou goest, I will go; and where thou lodgest, I will lodge" (Ruth 1:16). But I took only one with me. He proved a good servant and is, I believe, a true follower of our blessed Jesus.

Counting the Hours

The people of Bristol insisted upon my coming there again. Since my sailing was further delayed, I paid them a second visit on May 23. Multitudes came to meet me outside the city, some on foot, others in coaches. Almost all saluted and blessed me as I went along the street.

In Bristol I received letters from London informing me that my ship would not embark for two months. This news gladdened many hearts but not mine, for I was counting the hours until I could go abroad. I continued preaching, as usual, about five times a week. As the meetings progressed, the congregations grew larger and larger. It was wonderful to see how the people hung upon the rails of the organ loft, climbed upon the leads of the church, and made the church itself so hot with their breath that the steam would fall from the pillars like drops of rain. Sometimes for lack of room almost as many would go away as came in. It was with great difficulty that I got to the pulpit to read prayers or preach. Persons of all denominations and rank flocked to hear me, not only attending my ministry but giving me private invitations to their homes. From those meetings a new society or two were started. I preached and collected for the needs of the poor prisoners in Newgate two to three times a week. Many made me large offers if I would not go to America.

During my stay in Bristol, I paid another visit to Bath. I also preached three times in the Abbey Church and once in Queen's Chapel. People crowded in and were as affected as at Bristol. God stirred up some elect ladies to give over one hundred sixty pounds for the poor.

Early Morning Escape

On June 21, I said my last farewell at Bristol. When I came to tell the congregation that they would see my face no more, they all burst into a flood of tears such as I had never seen before. After the sermon, multitudes followed me home, weeping. I spent the next day from seven in the morning till midnight talking and giving spiritual advice to awakened souls.

About three the following morning, having thrown myself on the bed for an hour or two, I set out for Gloucester because I had heard that a great company on horseback and in coaches intended to see me out of town. Some were so disappointed that they followed me to Gloucester. I stayed a few days and preached to a very crowded congregation. From there I went on to Oxford where we had a general meeting of the Methodists. I found them flourishing. But I was impatient to go abroad, so I hastened away after a most affectionate visit, arriving in London about the end of August.

Until I embarked, every hour seemed a week and every week a year. I knew there was no minister at Frederica where I was then appointed, and I did not care to be absent any longer from my proper charge. Having now taken a final farewell of all my friends in the country, I was resolved to stay in London and give myself wholly to prayer and the study of the Scriptures till we could embark.

Unexpected Provision

One day I paid a visit to a worthy doctor of divinity near London who introduced me to some Christian ladies who delighted in doing good. It was my practice to nourish my acquaintance with the rich for the benefit of the poor. I recommended two poor clergymen and another pious person to their charity. They said little, but between them gave about thirty-six guineas.

When we came to the doctor's house and he saw the ladies' generosity, he said, "If you had not spoken for others, you would have had a good deal of that yourself." But God gave me joy in having nothing and the poor having all.

Upon my return to London the next day, the first letter I opened contained a bank note for ten pounds, a present for me from an unexpected source. This encouraged me to go on doing good to others, with full assurance that the Lord would not leave me in want. Blessed be His name. I have many such instances of His tender concern for my temporal, as well as my eternal, welfare.

A Printed Defense

About this time, through the pleadings of friends and criticism of enemies, I was prevailed upon to print my sermon "The Nature and Necessity of our Regeneration, or New Birth, in

Christ Jesus," which God used to begin the awakening in London, Bristol, Gloucester, and Gloucestershire. The Dissenters, I found, were surprised to see a sermon on this subject from a clergyman of the Church of England. This sermon sold well to persons of all denominations both at home and abroad. I soon had to order a second printing. Another of my sermons was very inaccurately printed without my permission at Bristol. I was obliged to publish in my own defense. Afterward, I sensed a clear call to print any other discourses I found helpful to the good of souls.

Being determined to reside in London till the time of my departure, I followed my usual practice of reading and praying over the Word of God upon my knees. This was sweet retirement for my soul. But it did not last long. I was soon invited to preach at Cripplegate, St. Ann's, and Forster Lane churches, at six on Sunday morning and to assist in administering holy communion. I accepted the invitations. So many came that sometimes we were obliged to consecrate fresh communion elements two or three times because it was difficult for stewards to carry all the offerings to the communion table.

Joy Unspeakable

I also preached at Wapping Chapel, the Tower, Ludgate, Newgate, and many of the churches where weekly lectures were held. The congregations continually increased. On a Lord's Day, I generally used to preach four times to a very large and responsive congregation, besides reading prayers two or three times and walking perhaps twelve miles from one church to the other. But God made my feet like hinds' feet and filled me with joy unspeakable at the end of my day's work. This made me see that my friends' advice to spare myself was a temptation. I found by daily experience that the more I did, the more I could do for God.

About the end of August, finding there were many young men from religious societies who attended my meetings, I entered one of their singing societies, hoping to have greater opportunities of reaching them. The Lord allowed me to bring spiritual truth to the singing groups. After they had taught me their repertoire scale they gladly let me teach them some of the mysteries of the new birth and the necessity of living for God. We spent many nights together in this way. Afterward many of these youths, to all appearances, walked with God. I trust they will join in the heavenly choir in singing praises to the Lamb and Him who sits on the throne forever.

Headlines in the Newspaper

About the middle of September, my name first appeared in the public newspapers. The Sunday before, I was asked to preach a charity sermon at Wapping Chapel. The congregation was very large, and more was collected than had been for many years on such an occasion. My friends entreated me to preach another charity sermon at Sir George Wheeler's Chapel. Through their pleadings, I agreed to do it. I discoursed upon the widow's giving her two mites. God bowed the hearts of the hearers as one. Almost all, as I was told by the ushers, offered most willingly. The Sunday following, I preached in the evening at St. Swithin's, where eight pounds instead of ten shillings were collected.

The next morning as I was at breakfast with a friend at the Tower, I read in one of the newspapers that "there was a young gentleman going voluntarily to Georgia. He had preached at St. Swithin's and collected eight pounds instead of ten shillings, three pounds of which were in half-pence. He was to preach the next Wednesday before the societies at their general quarterly meeting." This advertisement chagrined me. I immediately wrote to the editor asking him not to put me in his paper anymore. His answer was that he was paid for doing it, and that he would not lose two shillings for anybody. By this means, people's curiosity was stirred up more and more.

The Churches Are Too Small

On Wednesday evening, Bow Church in Cheapside was exceedingly crowded. I preached my sermon on "Early Piety" and at the request of the societies, printed it. For the next three successive months, there was no end of the people flocking to hear the Word of God. The church wardens and managers of charity schools were continually asking me to preach for the benefit of the children. As I was to embark shortly, they procured the use of churches on weekdays, a thing never done before. My appointment book sometimes had names of more than a dozen different churches at which I had promised to preach. When I preached, constables had to be placed at the door to keep the people in order. The sight of the congregations was awesome. Thousands went away from the largest churches for lack of room. They gave their full attention, listening like people concerned for eternity.

I now preached nine times a week. The early communions were awesome. On Sunday mornings, long before day, you might see streets filled with people going to church. With lanterns in their hands, they conversed about the things of God. Other lecture churches nearby would be filled with persons who could not come where I was preaching. Those who did come were as deeply affected as persons struck with pointed arrows, or mourning the loss of a firstborn child. People gave so liberally to the charity schools that nearly one thousand pounds sterling was collected at several churches. Many private contributions and subscriptions were also sent in afterward. I always preached without fee.

The orphan boys and girls looked upon me as their great benefactor. They frequently sent up their infant prayers in my behalf. William Seward, their hearty friend and advocate, was concerned with more than twenty charity schools. Some months afterward I discovered he had inserted the newspaper paragraph that so chagrined me.

The tide of popularity began to run very high. I could no

longer walk on foot as usual, but had to go in a coach from place to place to avoid the hosannas of the multitude. They grew quite extravagant in their applause. Had it not been for my compassionate Jesus, popularity would have destroyed me. I used to plead with Him to take me by the hand and lead me unhurt through this fiery furnace. He heard my request and allowed me to see the vanity of all applause except His own.

The Clergy Turn Sour

But all did not speak well of me. As my popularity increased, opposition also increased. At first, many of the clergy were my admirers, but some soon grew angry and complained that the churches were so crowded that there was no room for the parishioners and that the pews were being soiled. Some called me a spiritual pickpocket. Others thought I used a charm to get the people's money. One rumor spread that the Bishop of London, upon the complaint of the clergy, intended to silence me. I immediately visited him and inquired whether any complaint of this nature had been lodged against me. He answered, "No." I asked him whether any objection could be made against my doctrine. He said, "No," for he knew a clergyman who had heard me preach a plain spiritual sermon. I asked him to grant me a license. He said I needed none since I was going to Georgia. I replied, "Then you do not forbid my preaching?" He gave me a satisfactory answer and I left.

Soon after this, two clergyman told me they would not let me preach in their pulpits anymore unless I renounced that part of my sermon on rebirth. I suggested that they preach more often on the new birth. I said I had no freedom to do as they asked, so they continued to oppose.

Eating with Publicans and Sinners

Some of my enemies were irritated more because of my free conversation with many of the serious nonchurchmen than anything. These men invited me to their houses and repeatedly assured me that if the doctrine of the new birth and justification by faith was preached powerfully in the Church of England, there would be few Dissenters. I thought association with them was quite agreeable to the Word of God. Their conversation was savory. I imagined the best way to bring them over was not by bigotry and railing but by moderation, love, and holiness of life. But these reasons were of no avail.

One minister called me a "pragmatical rascal" and vehemently criticized all of those outside the church. This stirred up the people. Having a great fondness for me, some would leave whenever they came to church and found that I would not be preaching. I always endeavored to quell this spirit, writing a sermon purposely from the words, "Take heed therefore how ye hear" (Luke 8:18). One time a church warden intended to fine his parish minister eight pounds a year because he refused to let me preach there. I composed a sermon on "Love your enemies" and delivered it where I knew the church warden would be. It had its desired effect. He spoke to me after the service and told me he was convinced by my sermon that he should not resent the injury the minister had done me, and then thanked me for my care.

My Weakness in Opposition

Nor was I without opposition from friends who were jealous over me with a godly jealousy. My sermons were everywhere called for. News came from time to time of the springing up and increase of the seed sown in Bristol, Gloucester, and elsewhere. Large offers were made to me so I would stay in England. All the opposition I met, joined with the consciousness of my daily infirmities, was not enough ballast to keep me from overturning.

However, the Lord was pleased to be with me and bless me day by day. I had a nucleus of religious friends with whom I attempted to pray. Later, I think in October, we began to set apart an hour every evening to intercede with God to carry on the work and for the circle of our acquaintance according to their needs. I was their mouth to God, and He alone knows what encouragement I felt in that divine employment. Once we spent a whole night in prayer and praise. Many a time, at midnight or one in the morning, being wearied almost to death from preaching, writing, conversation, and travel, God imparted new life to my soul. He enabled me to intercede with Him for one and a half to two hours. The wonder of this communion made me compose my sermon on intercession. I do not think it presumption to suppose that it was in answer to these prayers by His children, that the Word, for some years now, has run and been glorified, not only in England but also in many other parts of the world.

Painting His Image on My Heart

I think it was at this time that I was prevailed on to sit for a portrait. The occasion was this. Some mischievous person had painted me leaning on a cushion, with a bishop looking very enviously over my shoulder. At the bottom a line stated that the bishops were "Mitred Drones." The artist attested in the papers that I had posed for it. I looked upon this as a snare of the devil to incense the clergy against me. I consulted friends about what to do. They told me I must sit for a picture in my own defense. At the same time, my aged mother commanded me to do so in a letter, urging that if I would not let her have the substance, I could at least leave her the shadow. She also named a painter. I accidentally met him one night, and with great reluctance I complied. While the painter was drawing my face, I endeavored to employ my time in beseeching the great God, by His Holy Spirit, to paint His blessed image upon the artist's and my hearts.

"Brethren, Farewell!"

Christmas was near. I received notice that we were almost ready to embark for Georgia. I resolved to throw myself into the hands of God and go. The nearer the time of my departure approached, the more affectionate and eager the people grew. There was no end of persons coming to me with soul concern. I preached and God blessed me more and more and sustained me for some time with very little sleep.

I departed at the beginnning of Christmas week. What groans and sighs were to be heard when I said, "Finally, brethren, farewell!" At Great St. Helen's the cry was amazing. It took nearly half an hour to leave. All ranks gave vent to their passions. Thousands and thousands of prayers were offered for me. People would run and stop me in the alleys, hug me in their arms, and follow me with wishful looks. Before my departure, I spent a night with many others in prayer and praise. In the morning, I helped administer communion at St. Dunstan's. But I never before saw such a service. The tears of the communicants mingled with the wine. Had Jesus not comforted our tears, our parting would have almost been unbearable.

Finally, on December 28, I boarded the *Whitaker* after having preached in many of the London churches, collected from friends about a thousand pounds for the charity schools and over three hundred pounds for the poor of Georgia. At the same time God provided enough to supply my own temporal needs and gave me repeated proofs that if we seek first the Kingdom of God and His righteousness, all other things shall be added unto us. For these, and all His other unmerited mercies, I desire to praise Him and magnify His holy name through the boundless ages of eternity.

Let me exhort you. If you are a serious child of God, bless Him for what He has done for my soul. If you are still in the gall of bitterness and think that I have either not told the truth or written out of a vainglorious view, let me ask you to suspend your judgment for a little while and allow Jesus to decide the question. At His tribunal we shall meet, and there you shall know what is in my heart and what the motives were which led me out into such a way of life.

Part 2

The Divine Enabling for Revival

4

*John Wesley: Miracles Begin**

In mid-September 1738, I returned from visiting the Moravians in Germany and began again to declare in my own country the glad tidings of salvation. I preached three times and afterward expounded the Holy Scripture to a large congregation in the Minories. I rejoiced to meet with our little society, which had grown to thirty-two persons.

Immediately, I went to the condemned felons in Newgate and offered them free salvation. In the evening I went to a society in Bear Yard and preached repentance and remission of sins. The next evening I spoke the truth in love at a society in Aldersgate Street.

I was emboldened to speak strongly at Newgate, at the society, the next day at St. Anne's, and twice at St. John's, in Clerkenwell. I spoke so strongly, I fear they will not allow me to return.

October began on a Sunday and I preached both morning and afternoon at St. George's, in the east. At week's end, I preached at St. Antholin's once more. One afternoon I went to

---

*Nehemiah Curnock, *op. cit.,* pp. 61–73, September 17, 1738 through May 31, 1739.

the rector to tell him, between us alone, of the injury he had done both to God and me by preaching and printing that very weak sermon on assurance. The assurance we preach is of quite another kind from the one he writes about. We speak of the assurance of our present pardon, but he wrote only of our final perseverance.

On Monday I set out for Oxford. While walking, I read the truly surprising narrative of the conversions lately wrought in and about the town of Northhampton in New England.

November found me settled back in London. There I preached Sunday morning at St. Botolph's, Bishopgate, in the afternoon at Islington, and in the evening to the largest congregation I ever saw at St. Clement's, in the Strand. This was the first time that I preached here and I suppose it is to be the last.

Last Rites at the Prison

That week Charles and I went to do the last rites of the condemned prisoners at their request. It was the most glorious instance I ever saw of faith triumphing over sin and death. Charles took that occasion to declare the gospel of peace to the large assembly of prisoners and other sinners.

The next Sunday I preached twice at the prison. In the following week, I began carefully to inquire what the doctrine of the Church of England is concerning the controversial point of justification by faith. I extracted and printed what I found useful for others.

As December came, I began reading prayers, which had been long discontinued, at Bocardo, the city jail. In the afternoon, I received a letter earnestly requesting me to publish my account of Georgia, and another, just as earnest, dissuading me from it "because it would bring much trouble upon me." I consulted God in His Word and received two answers: the first, Ezekiel 33:2-6; the other, "Thou therefore endure hardness, as a good soldier of Jesus Christ" (2 Tim. 2:3).

Later, at St. Thomas's, there was a young woman who was raving mad, screaming and continually tormenting herself. I had a strong desire to speak to her. The moment I began she was still. The tears ran down her cheeks all the time I was telling her, "Jesus of Nazareth is able and willing to deliver you."

By mid-December, George Whitefield arrived from Georgia. I hastened to London to see him. God once more gave us wonderful counsel together.

Knocked to the Ground in Prayer

At New Year's 1739, George Whitefield, my brother Charles, three others and I, with about sixty of our brethren, were present at a love feast in Fetter Lane. About three in the morning, as we were continuing in prayer, the power of God came upon us so mightily that many cried out in holy joy, while others were knocked to the ground. As soon as we were recovered a little from awe and amazement at the presence of God, we broke out in one voice, "We praise Thee, O God; we acknowledge Thee to be the Lord."

On the evening of the third Sunday of January, while I was preaching in the Minories, a well-dressed, middle-aged woman suddenly cried out as if in the agony of death. She continued to do so for some time, with all the signs of sharp anguish of spirit. When she was a little recovered, I asked her to call upon me the next day, which she did.

She told me that about three years before, she had been under strong conviction of sin and in terror of mind. She had no comfort in anything nor any rest day or night. She had sent for the minister of her parish and related to him the distress she suffered. The minister told her husband she was stark mad, and advised him to send for a physician immediately. The physician ordered her to be bled, blistered, and so on. All this did not heal her wounded spirit. She continued in her distress until she found deliverance through Jesus Christ the day she came to see me. He whose word she at first found to be sharper than any two-edged sword gave her hope that He would heal her sinful soul.

Trying the Spirits

At the end of January, having been long encouraged to do so, I went with four or five of my friends to a house where there was a woman called a Christian prophet. After a while, she entered the room where we were waiting. She appeared to be about twenty-four or twenty-five, and spoke and behaved in an agreeable manner. When she asked us why we came, I said "To try the spirits, to see if they are of God." She immediately leaned back in her chair and seemed to have strong workings in her mind.

She spoke much, mostly in Scripture, of the fulfilling of prophecies, the coming of Christ now at hand, and the spreading of the Gospel over all the earth. Two or three of our company were much affected and believed she spoke by the Spirit of God. But this was in no way clear to me. The prophecy might be either hysterical or artificial. Any person with a good understanding of the Scriptures might have spoken the same words. But I let the matter alone, believing that if it was not of God, it would come to naught.

An Opposer Finds Forgiveness

It was the advice of all our brethren that I should spend a few days at Oxford. I accordingly went on Saturday, March 3. One of the most surprising instances of God's power that I ever remember having seen happened on the following Tuesday. I visited one who was extremely enraged at our "new way" and zealous in opposing it. Finding that argument only inflamed her more and more, I broke off the dispute and asked that we might join in prayer. She consented to kneel down. In a few minutes she fell into an extreme agony, both of body and soul, and soon after cried out with the utmost earnestness, "Now I know I am forgiven for Christ's sake."

On Thursday I called on her and a few of her neighbors, who met together in the evening. Among these I found a gentleman of the same contentious spirit, earnestly laboring to pervert the truth of the Gospel. To prevent his going on, as the lesser of the two evils, I entered directly into the controversy, discussing both the cause and the fruits of justification. In the midst of the dispute, one of the ladies present felt as if she were pierced by a sword. Before she could be brought to another house, where I was going, she could not avoid loudly crying out, even in the street. But no sooner had we made our request to God than He sent her peace from His holy place.

The next Saturday afternoon, I traveled to Dummer. On Sunday morning I had a large and attentive congregation. The next day I returned to Reading, and then on Tuesday to Oxford, where I found many rejoicing in God their Savior more and more. I left Oxford early Thursday morning, arriving in London in the afternoon.

Called Out of London

During my stay in London, I was constantly busy. Between our own society in Fetter Lane and many others where I was continually asked to speak, I had no thought of leaving London. There I received a letter from George Whitefield entreating me to come to Bristol without delay.

This I was not at all interested in doing, but I submitted the invitation to our society in Fetter Lane. My brother Charles could hardly bear the mention of it. Appealing to the Word of God, he received these words as spoken to himself, and objected no more, "Son of man, behold, I take away from thee the desire of thine eyes with a stroke: yet neither shalt thou mourn nor weep, neither shall thy tears run down" (Ezek. 24:16).

Our brethren, however, continued the dispute without any probability of their coming to one conclusion. At length we all agreed to decide it by lot, and by this it was determined I should go.

A Strange Way of Preaching

In the evening of March 31, I reached Bristol, where I met George Whitefield. I could scarcely reconcile myself at first to his strange way of preaching—in the fields. Having all my life been so careful of every point relating to decency and order, I almost thought the saving of souls a sin if it had not taken place in a church.

So, Sunday evening, April 1, George Whitefield having left me to go it alone, I began expounding our Lord's Sermon on the Mount to a little society which was accustomed to meeting once or twice a week in Nicholas Street.

The following Monday at four in the afternoon, I submitted to being more vile, as I thought it, and proclaimed in the highways the glad tidings of salvation, speaking from a little hill adjoining the city to about three thousand people. The scripture on which I spoke was "The Spirit of the Lord is upon me, because he hath anointed me to preach the gospel to the poor; he hath sent me to heal the brokenhearted, to preach deliverance to the captives, and recovering of sight to the blind, to set at liberty them that are bruised, to preach the acceptable year of the Lord" (Luke 4:18–19).

At seven I began expounding the Acts of the Apostles to a society meeting in Baldwin Street, and the next day the Gospel of John in the chapel at Newgate, where I also daily read the morning service of the Church.

On Wednesday, at Baptist Mills, a sort of suburb or village about half a mile from Bristol, I offered the grace of God to about fifteen hundred persons from these words, "I will heal their backsliding, I will love them freely" (Hosea 14:4).

In the evening three women agreed to meet together weekly, with the same intention as those at London: to confess their faults one to another and pray for one another that they might be healed. Four young men agreed to meet for the same purpose. How dare any man deny this to be a means of grace ordained by God!

On Thursday, at five in the evening, I began expounding on Romans at a society in Castle Street. The next evening I taught John 1 at a society in Gloucester Lane. On Saturday evening, at Weaver's Hall, I began teaching the Epistle to the Romans and declared the Gospel, which is the "power of God unto salvation to every one that believeth" (Rom. 1:16), to all.

Offering Grace to Thousands

The second Sunday of the month, at seven in the morning, I preached to about a thousand persons at Bristol, and afterward to about fifteen hundred on top of Hannam Mount in Kingswood. I called to them, in the words of the evangelical prophet, "Ho, every one that thirsteth, come ye to the waters, and he that hath no money; come ye, buy, and eat; yea, come, buy wine and milk without money and without price" (Isa. 55:1). About five thousand were at Rose Green, on the other side of Kingswood, in the afternoon. I stood among them and cried, in the name of the Lord, "If any man thirst, let him come unto me, and drink" (John 7:37).

On Tuesday, I went to Bath, where I offered about a thousand souls the free grace of God to "heal their backsliding" (Hosea 14:4). The next morning, I believe there were more than two thousand who listened. I preached to about the same number at Baptist Mills in the afternoon.

Saturday I preached at the poorhouse. Three or four hundred were inside, and more than twice that number outside. To them I explained those encouraging words: "When they had nothing to pay, he frankly forgave them both" (Luke 7:42).

Later I explained the story of the Pharisee and the Publican to five and six thousand persons. About three thousand were present at Hannam Mount. I preached at Newgate after dinner to a crowded congregation. Between five and six we went to

Rose Green, where it rained hard, but not a drop fell upon us while I declared to about five thousand, "Christ, our wisdom, righteousness, sanctification and redemption." I concluded the day by showing at the society in Baldwin Street that Jesus' blood "cleanseth us from all sin" (1 John 1:7).

The following Tuesday, at five in the afternoon, I was at a little society in the Back Lane. The room in which we were holding the meeting was propped underneath, but the weight of the people made the floor give way. As I had begun preaching, the post which propped the floor fell down with a great noise, but the floor sank no farther. After the sudden surprise, all settled down and quietly attended to the words being spoken.

God Confirms His Word

From Back Lane I went to Baldwin Street and preached on the fourth chapter of Acts. After delivering the message, I called upon God to confirm His word. Immediately, to my surprise, someone nearby cried out with the utmost vehemence, as though in agony of death. We continued in prayer till a new song was put into her mouth and thanksgiving unto our God. Soon after, two other persons were seized with strong pain and constrained to cry for the restlessness of their hearts. But it was not long before they likewise burst forth into praise to God as their Savior. The last who called upon God, as out of the belly of hell, was a stranger in Bristol. In a short time he was also overwhelmed with joy and love, knowing that God had healed his backslidings.

Wednesday evening, a few were admitted into the society, among them a former Quaker who had been baptized the day before. One person was scarcely able either to speak or look up. The sorrows of death compassed her and the pains of hell got hold of her. We poured out our prayers before God and showed Him her trouble. He soon revealed himself as a God who hears prayer. She soon felt the peace of God through Jesus Christ and rejoiced in the hope of the glory of God. Now the love of God was shed abroad in her heart.

The next Saturday at Weaver's Hall a young man was suddenly seized with a violent trembling. In a few minutes, the sorrows of his heart increased and he sank down to the ground. We never ceased calling upon God till He raised him up full of peace and joy in the Holy Spirit.

After repeated invitations, I went to Pensford, about five miles from Bristol. I wrote to the minister, asking permission to preach in the church. After waiting some time and receiving no answer, I preached to many of the people gathered together in an open place, calling out, "If any man thirst, let him come unto me and drink" (John 7:37). At four in the afternoon there were over three thousand in a convenient place near Bristol to whom I declared, "The hour is coming, and now is, when the dead shall hear the voice of the Son of God: and they that hear shall live" (John 5:25).

I also preached at Bath, to about a thousand on Tuesday morning, and at four in the afternoon to the poor coal miners at a place called Two-Mile-Hill in Kingswood. In the evening at Baldwin Street, a young man, after a sharp agony of body and mind, found his soul filled with peace, knowing in whom he had believed.

God Sets His Seal to His Word

Thursday, while I was preaching at Newgate on these words, "He that believeth on me hath everlasting life" (John 6:47), I was led to declare strongly and explicitly that God wills all men to be thus saved. I asked them to pray that if this was the will of God, He would bear witness to His word.

Immediately one, then another, and another sank to the earth. They dropped on every side as if thunderstruck. One cried aloud. We besought God in her behalf and He turned her heaviness into joy. A second being in the same agony, we called upon God for her also. He spoke peace unto her soul.

In the evening I was again pressed in spirit to declare, Christ "gave himself a ransom for all" (1 Tim. 2:6). Almost before we called upon God to set to His seal, He answered. One was so wounded by the sword of the Spirit that you would have imagined she could not live a moment. But soon His abundant kindness was revealed to her, and she loudly sang of His righteousness.

On Friday all Newgate rang with the cries of those whom the word of God had cut to the heart. Two of these were filled with joy in a moment, to the astonishment of those who watched them.

On the last Sunday in May, I declared the free grace of God to about four thousand people. I then went to Clifton, a mile from Bristol, to visit a minister who was extremely ill. I returned to a little plain near Hannam Mount, where about three thousand were present. After dinner I went to Clifton again. The church was quite full at the prayers and sermon, as was the churchyard at a burial which followed. From Clifton we went to Rose Green where we counted nearly seven thousand.

The Work of the Spirit Is Questioned

By the end of April, we understood that many were offended at the cries of those on whom the power of God came. One of these was a physician who was afraid these cases might be fraud. Today while I was preaching at Newgate, one whom the doctor had known for many years was the first who broke out into strong cries and tears. The physician could hardly believe his own eyes and ears. He went over and stood close to her, observing every symptom, till great drops of sweat ran down her face and her entire body shook. He did not know what to think, being clearly convinced it was not fraud nor any natural disorder. But when both her soul and body were healed in a moment, he acknowledged the work of God.

By May many more than before were offended. At Baldwin Street my voice could scarcely be heard amid the groanings of some and the cries of others, calling aloud to Him who is able to save.

A Quaker who stood by was greatly displeased at the commotion and was biting his lips and scowling angrily. Suddenly he dropped down as if thunderstruck. The agony he was in was terrible to behold. We begged God not to charge him with his folly. God answered and the man soon lifted his head and cried aloud, "Now I know you are a prophet of the Lord!"

At Newgate another mourner was comforted. I was asked to step into a house to read a letter written against me. The letter stated that I was a deceiver of the people because I taught that God wills all men to be saved. One person who had long asserted the contrary was there when a young woman came in. Just as we rose from giving thanks, she reeled four or five steps, then dropped down. We prayed for her and left her strongly convinced of sin, earnestly groaning for deliverance.

"This Is He Who I Said Was a Deceiver of People."

The night before, at Baldwin Street, there was a weaver— a man of normal activity and behavior, one who constantly attended the public prayers and was zealous for the church, standing against Dissenters of every denomination. Hearing that people fell into strange fits at the societies, he had come to see and judge for himself. But he was less satisfied than before. He went about to his friends, one after another, and labored to convince them that this phenomena was a delusion of the devil.

On our way home, someone met us in the street and informed us that the weaver had fallen down, raving mad. The weaver had sat down to dinner but decided to first finish reading a sermon he had borrowed on "Salvation by Faith." While reading the last page, he changed color, fell off his chair, and began screaming terribly as he beat himself against the ground. The neighbors were alarmed and flocked together in his house. Between one and two in the morning, I came in and found him on the floor. The room was full of people whom his wife tried to keep out. He cried aloud, "No, let them all come! Let all the world see the just judgment of God!"

Two or three men were trying to hold him down. He immediately fixed his eyes on me, stretched out his hand, and cried, "Aye, this is he who I said was a deceiver of people! But God has overtaken me. I said it was all a delusion, but this is no delusion." He then roared out, "Oh, you devil! You cursed devil! Yes, you legion of devils! You cannot stay. Christ will cast you out. I know His work is done. Tear me to pieces if you will, but you cannot hurt me!"

He then beat himself to the ground again, his breast heaving at the same time, as though in the pangs of death, with great drops of sweat trickling down his face. We all began praying. His pangs ceased, and both his body and soul were set at liberty.

Barred from the Churches

The next Monday, as I was preparing to set out for Pensford, now having permission to preach in the church, I received a note:

> Sir: Our minister, having been informed you are beside yourself, does not care to have you preach in any of his churches.

However, I went, and on Priest Down, about half a mile from Pensford, preached "Christ our wisdom, righteousness, sanctification and redemption."

My ordinary employment was now a busy schedule. Every morning I read prayers and preached at Newgate. Every evening I taught a portion of Scripture at one or more of the societies. On Monday afternoon I preached abroad near Bristol, on Tuesday at Bath and Two-Mile-Hill alternately, on Wednesday at Baptist Mills, near Pensford, every other Thursday, then every other Friday in another part of Kingswood. On Saturday afternoon and Sunday morning I preached in the Bowling

Green, and on Sunday at eleven near Hannam Mount, at two at Clifton, and at five at Rose Green. As my days are, so is my strength.

On Sunday the 20th, seeing many of the rich at Clifton church, my heart was much pained for them. I earnestly desired that some of them might enter into the kingdom of heaven. But full of the Spirit as I was, I did not know where to begin in warning them to flee from the wrath to come till my Testament opened on these words: "I came not to call the righteous, but sinners to repentance" (Mark 2:17). In applying this, my soul was so encouraged that I could have cried out, "Give me a place to stand, and I will shake the earth!"

When I preached at Rose Green, God's sending lightning with the rain did not hinder fifteen hundred from staying. In the evening as I was preaching, God spoke to three whose souls were all storm and tempest, and immediately there was a great calm.

Our Lord Answers for Himself

While I was enforcing these words, "Be still, and know that I am God" (Ps. 46:10), God began to bare His arm, not in private, but in the open air and before more than two thousand witnesses. One, then another, and yet another was struck to the earth, greatly trembling at the presence of God's power. Others loudly and bitterly cried, "What must we do to be saved?" In less than an hour, seven persons, wholly unknown to me till that time, were rejoicing, singing, and giving thanks to the God of their salvation with all their might.

One evening at Nicholas Street, I was interrupted almost as soon as I had begun to speak by the cries of one who was pricked at the heart. He strongly groaned for pardon and peace. I went on to declare what God had already done to prove that He is "not willing that any should perish, but that all should come to repentance" (2 Pet. 3:9). Another person dropped down close to one who was strongly opposed to my doctrine. While he stood astonished at the sight, a little boy near him was seized in the same manner. A young man who stood behind fixed his eyes on him and sank down as if dead. He soon began to cry out and beat himself against the ground so that six men could scarcely hold him. His name was Thomas Maxfield. I never saw more than one other so torn by the evil one. Meanwhile, many others began to cry out to the Savior for help, because all the house and all the street was in an uproar. We continued in prayer. Before ten the greater part found rest for their souls.

Later I was escorted from supper to someone who had run out of the society in all haste that she might not expose herself, having been more deeply convicted of sin than ever. But the hand of God followed her. After going a few steps, she was forced to be carried home. When she was there, she grew worse and worse and was in a violent agony by the time we came. We called upon God, and her soul found rest.

About twelve I was begged to go and visit one more person. She had only one struggle after I came, and was then filled with peace and joy. I think twenty-nine in all received the Holy Spirit that day.

I also preached to about a thousand at Bath. There were several young prostitutes among them, to whom I especially called, "Awake thou that sleepest! Arise from the dead, and Christ shall give thee light."

The next day I preached at Rose Green to the largest congregation I had ever had there, perhaps about ten thousand. I used the scripture, "Ye know not what manner of spirit ye are of, for the Son of man is not come to destroy men's lives, but to save them" (Luke 9:55–56). At the society in the evening, eleven were deeply convinced of sin and soon after received their forgiveness.

5

George Whitefield: In The Strength of Christ*

Friday, December 8, 1738, I returned to London about noon and was received with much joy by my Christian friends for my safe arrival. In the evening I went to a truly Christian society in Fetter Lane and perceived God had greatly watered the seed sown by my ministry when last in London. *Lord, increase it more and more!* The following morning I met with the Archbishop of Canterbury and the Bishop of London, having a favorable reception.

When I was on board the *Mary* returning home, parts of Jeremiah relating to the opposition he met from the false prophets were deeply impressed upon me. Now I begin to see the wisdom of God in my own situation, for five churches have already been denied me. Some of the clergy, if possible, would have me leave. But I rejoice in this opposition, because I believe it is a certain sign that a more effectual door will be opened, since there are so many adversaries.

---

*George Whitefield, *op. cit.,* "The Third Journal," pp. 116–177, December 1738 through June 1739.

A Great Outpouring of the Spirit

However, I had an opportunity to preach with great power to large congregations in the morning at St. Helen's and at Islington in the afternoon. There seems to be a great outpouring of the Spirit, and many who were awakened by my preaching a year ago have now grown into strong men in Christ by the ministrations of my friends and fellow laborers, John and Charles Wesley. Blessed be God! I rejoice in the coming of the Kingdom of His dear Son.

The old doctrine about justification by faith alone is well received. Many letters had been sent to me concerning the teaching. I'm glad I providentially missed them all. Now I come unprejudiced and can more easily see who is right. Who dare assert that we are not justified in the sight of God merely by an act of faith in Jesus Christ, without any regard to works past, present, or future?

In the evening I went to Fetter Lane Society, where we had a love feast, eating a little bread and water and spending about two hours in singing and prayers. I found my heart greatly united with the brethren. Surely a primitive spirit is reviving among us.

The next Sunday I preached twice, once in the evening at Crooked Lane Society. There God enabled me to withstand several persons who argued against the doctrine of the new birth. The passion with which they oppose it is a demonstration that they themselves have not experienced salvation. *Lord, make them partakers of it, for Jesus' sake.*

After I left Crooked Lane, I went to Little Britain and expounded to a group there. Then I went to another love feast at Fetter Lane. Since it was Christmas Eve, we continued till nearly four in the morning in prayer, psalms, and thanksgiving. My heart was released and full of love among these Christian brethren. God gave me a great spirit of supplication, adoring His free grace in Christ Jesus.

About four the next morning, I went to another society in

Redcross Street, where I prayed and expounded to about two to three hundred people. I had been watching in prayer all night, and God so filled me with His blessed Spirit that I spoke with greater power than I ever did in my life. My body was weak but I found supernatural strength and the truth of that saying, "When I am weak, then am I strong."

At six I went to Crutched Friars Society and expounded as well as I could, but perceived myself a little oppressed with drowsiness. How the corruptible body does weigh down the soul. When shall I be delivered from the burden of this flesh?

I preached three times and assisted in administering communion at the same time. Christmas, twenty-four years ago today, I was baptized. *Lord, to what little purpose have I lived?* However, I sealed my baptismal covenant with my dear Savior's blessed Body and Blood, and trust in His strength to keep me performing His will.

"The Kingdom of God is within Me"

The last week in December I preached nine times and expounded nearly eighteen times, with great power and freedom. I am employed every moment from morning till midnight. There is no end to the number of people coming or sending for me, and they seem more and more desirous, like newborn babes, to be fed with the sincere milk of the Word. What a great work has been wrought in the hearts of many this past year! Now I know that even though thousands might come at first out of curiosity, yet God has quickened them by His free grace. Oh, that I could be humble and thankful!

Glory be to God that He fills me continually, not only with peace but also joy in the Holy Spirit. Before my arrival, I thought I should envy my brethren's success in the ministry, but blessed be God, I rejoice in it and am glad to see Christ's kingdom come. Sometimes I feel myself deserted for a little while and much oppressed, especially before preaching, but comfort soon flows in. The Kingdom of God is within me. Free grace in Christ is wonderful!

January 1, 1739, I received communion, preached twice, and expounded twice and found this to be the happiest New Year's Day I had ever yet seen. At night I had a love feast again with our brethren at Fetter Lane, and spent the whole night in close prayer, psalms, and thanksgiving. God supported me without sleep. Oh, that our despisers were partakers of our joys!

The following day I stayed home on purpose to receive those who wanted to consult me. From seven in the morning till three in the afternoon, people came—some telling me what God had done for their souls, and others crying out, "What shall I do to be saved?" God enabled me to give them answers of peace. How God does work by my unworthy hands! His mercies melt me down.

Thursday, January 4, a cold I had contracted seemed worse and I feared it would prevent my speaking, yet God enabled me to expound with power in a private society, and then to preach at Wapping Chapel, so that the Word pierced the hearers' souls. Afterward I expounded and prayed for an hour and a half with power and demonstration of the Spirit. My heart was indeed full of God. How immediately does Jesus Christ reward me for my poor services! As soon as my daily work is done, He says, "Enter thou into the joy of the Lord."

Convinced of God's Work Among Us

On January 5, I held a conference at Islington with seven true ministers of Jesus Christ, despised Methodists whom God has brought together. What we were in doubt about, after prayer, we determined by lot. Everything else was carried on with great love, meekness, and devotion. We continued in fasting and prayer till three o'clock and then parted with a full conviction that God was going to do great things among us.

I did not find the pity I ought to have when seeing a brother full of self-love. *Lord, enlarge my narrow heart and give me that love which rejoices not in iniquity but in the truth!* I perceived something bordering on envy toward a brother. When shall I come to rejoice in others' gifts and graces as much as in my own? I am resolved to wrestle with Jesus Christ by faith and prayer till He gives me humility.

I expounded two or three times every night this week. The Holy Spirit so powerfully worked upon my hearers, pricking their hearts and melting them into such floods of tears that one spiritual man said he never saw the like before. God is truly with me. Adored be His unmerited goodness. I find His grace quickening me more and more every day. My understanding is more enlightened, my affections more inflamed, and my heart full of love toward God and man.

Though I sat up all Sunday night, God still carried me through the work of the day with only about an hour's sleep. I expounded in the evening and confuted a bitter opponent of the doctrine of the new birth and justification by faith alone. What can be said to those who will not be convinced? *Lord, open Thou their hearts and eyes.* I spent the remainder of the evening with our bands, little combinations of six or more Christians meeting together to compare their experiences and to build up one another. We confess our faults one to another and pray for one another that we may be healed.

I am staying at home again today to talk with those who came to consult me. I found that God has awakened several and excited in them a hunger and thirst after righteousness by my sermons on the power of Christ's resurrection and the words, "Have ye received the Holy Spirit?" Every day I hear of someone quickened to a sense of the divine life. What abundant reason I have to be thankful!

On Sunday, January 21, I preached twice with great power and clearness in my voice to two great congregations. Nearly a thousand people were gathered in the churchyard and hundreds more returned home that could not come in. God magnifies His power most when most opposed.

His Infinite Mercies

I expounded twice afterward, where the people pressed most vehemently to hear the Word. God enabled me to speak with the demonstration of the Spirit and with power. The remainder of the evening filled me with a humble sense of His infinite mercies. I think I am never more humble than when exalted.

God continues to enable me to speak on the doctrine of the new birth. However some might mock, others are affected—especially three Quakers who visited me and glorified God on my behalf. How thankful and humble I ought to be. God fills me with love, peace, and joy in the Holy Spirit by His free grace in Christ Jesus. The strength of God would surprise me if I did not know what a gracious Master I serve.

On Monday, January 29, I expounded twice. Then I sat up till nearly one in the morning with my honored brother and fellow-laborer, John Wesley. We debated with two clergymen from the Church of England and some other strong opposers of the doctrine of the new birth. God enabled me to declare with great simplicity what He had done for my soul. This made them look upon me as a madman. We speak about what we know and testify of that which we have seen, but they won't receive our witness. Now, therefore, I am fully convinced there is a fundamental difference between us and them. They believe only in an outward Christ. We believe that He must be inwardly formed in our hearts also. "But the natural man receiveth not the things of the Spirit of God: for they are foolishness unto him: neither can he know them, because they are spiritually discerned."

How God does deal with me! He gives me a heaven upon earth and makes my heart leap for joy almost continually. Oh, that all who now oppose us were partakers of this joy!

The first Sunday in February I preached in the morning at St. George's in the east. I preached again at Christ Church, Spitalfield's, and went to St. Margaret's, Westminster, where God enabled me to preach with greater power than I had all the day before.

Then I went to a love feast in Fetter Lane, where I spent the whole night in prayer and discussion of several important points with many truly Christian friends. About four in the morning we went and broke bread at a poor, sick sister's room. We parted, I hope, in a spirit like the early Christians.

This has been a wonderful Sabbath, indeed! God owned me before nearly twelve thousand people this day. How He has stengthened my body! How He has filled and satisfied my soul!

Satan Resists

The next Tuesday I went to St. Helen's, where Satan withstood me greatly. Suddenly my strength left me. I thought it was the devil's doing and, therefore, was resolved to resist him, steadfast in the faith. Accordingly, though I was exceedingly sick while reading the prayers, and almost unable to speak when I entered the pulpit, God gave me courage to begin. Before I had finished, I waxed warm and strong in the Spirit and offered Jesus Christ freely to all who would lay hold on Him by faith. I believe many were touched to the quick, for they seemed to feel what was spoken and said hearty and loud "Amen's" to my sentences. The church was crowded, and after I had finished, many prayed for my safe journey and return. Surely these are not curious hearers. If they are, why do they follow me more and more? No. Many conversions have been wrought in their hearts. God has set His seal to my ministry, and I trust these souls will be my joy and crown of rejoicing in the Day of the Lord Jesus.

After this, the people waited in great companies to see and follow me, but I got away from them by going out a back door. Hereafter, perhaps I may be enabled to escape in the same manner to avert the fury of my enemies.

At Basingstoke, in a large dining room in the public house, I gave notice that I would expound to as many as would come to hear me. In a short time I had above a hundred very attentive hearers. I expounded for over an hour, for which they were very thankful. Blessed be God for this opportunity! I hope I shall learn more and more every day that no place is amiss for preaching the Gospel. God forbid that the Word of God should be bound because some out of a misguided zeal deny the use of their churches. Though they bid me not to speak to the people in this way, I cannot but speak the things that I have seen and felt in my own heart. The more I am told to hold my tongue, the more earnestly will I lift up my voice like a trumpet and tell the people what must be done in them before they can be finally saved by Jesus Christ.

Persecution Proves My Ministry

The next evening I returned with my friends to Basingstoke, where I had promised to expound again. Accordingly, I went to a large room prepared for that purpose and spoke for an hour. The place was very crowded—many were very noisy and others did us the honor of throwing stones at the windows. I just spoke louder, convinced some good must come from a place of opposition. I would doubt I was a good minister of Christ if I were not opposed. Opposition does me much good, for it drives me nearer to my Lord and Master Jesus Christ, with whom I long to dwell.

Later, nearly twenty friends came to visit me. Two young men in particular came to question me about the doctrine of regeneration. Alas, they soon showed what strangers they were to it. One was so full of zeal that he could not keep his seat. Both were entirely ignorant of the indwelling of the Spirit and denied experience in religion. Poor men! I pitied and told them how they rested in so-called learning, while they were strangers to the power of godliness in their hearts. At last, finding no probability of convincing them, and being called for supper, I and my friends took our leave in love. Afterward we prayed for them and blessed God for making us triumphant through Jesus in every place.

On February 14, after dinner, I thought God called us to

Bristol. I reached that place about seven in the evening with cheerfulness of heart. Who can express the joy with which I was welcomed? I received many letters also from friends in London. My chief pleasure was that somebody thought me considerable enough to write a letter of opposition in the *Weekly Miscellany,* which included several untruths about my preaching at St. Margaret's, Westminster. *You shall answer for me, my Lord and my God.* A little while and we shall appear at the judgment seat of Christ. Then shall my innocence be made clear as the light.

"The Devil Is in You All."

At Bristol I received a letter from a dear Christian brother saying that an opposing minister had said, "I believe the devil in hell is in you all. Whitefield has set the town on fire, and now he is gone to kindle a flame in the country."

Shocking language for one who calls himself a minister of the Gospel! I trust this will not move us, unless it is to pity him and pray the more earnestly that he may experience the power of those truths he is now opposing, and have the same fire which he opposes kindled in his breast. I am persuaded mine is not a fire of the devil's kindling, but a holy fire. Oh, that such a fire may not only be kindled but blow up into flame all over England and the world!

After having breakfasted and prayed with some Christian friends, I called on the Rev. Mr. Gibbs, minister of St. Mary Redcliffe. I was informed he had promised to lend me his church for my preaching. But he refused, telling me that he could not lend his church without a special order from the chancellor.

I immediately went to see the chancellor. He told me frankly that he would not permit or prohibit any in lending me a church. He advised me to withdraw to some other place till he had heard from the bishop and not to preach on that or any other occasion. I asked him his reasons. He answered, "Why do you press me? It is a general dislike." I replied, "When was the

Gospel preached without dislike?"

I left him and then went to visit the dean, who received me with great civility. I asked him, " Could there be any just objection against my preaching in churches for the Georgia Orphan House?"

After a considerable pause, he answered he could not tell. When somebody knocked at the door, he replied, "Mr. Whitefield, I will give you an answer some other time. Now I expect company."

"Will you please fix a time, sir?" I asked.

"I will send for you," said the dean.

Oh, Christian simplicity, where have you fled? Why do the clergy not speak the truth? It is not against the Orphan House, but against me and my doctrine, that their enmity is leveled.

Sheep Without a Shepherd

About one in the afternoon the following Saturday, I went with two friends to Kingswood. I have long since yearned toward the many poor coal miners there. They are as sheep having no shepherd. After dinner I stood upon a mount and spoke to about two hundred who came to hear me. Blessed be God that I have now broken the ice. I believe I never was more acceptable to my Master than when I was standing to teach those hearers in the open fields. Some may censure me, but if I sought to please men, I would not be the servant of Christ.

Yesterday I thought I would not have the Sunday use of any pulpit. But God, who has the hearts of all men in His hands, disposed the Rev. Mr. Penrose to lend me his. He thanked me for my sermon, and the Rev. Mr. Gibbs sent to me and offered me the use both of St. Thomas's and St. Mary Redcliffe. The latter of these I accepted and preached with great liberty and demonstration of the Spirit to such a congregation as my eyes had never yet seen. Many went away exceedingly complimentary of me.

After my sermon I hastened to a society in Baldwin Street

where many hundreds were assembled to hear me. The stairs and court below, besides the room itself, were crowded. Here I expounded for almost two hours. Afterward I preached for the same length of time at another equally crowded society in Nicholas Street. Surely Jesus was with us, for great numbers were quite melted down. God so caused me to renew my strength that I was better when I returned home than when I began to exhort at six that morning. I could not do this except for Christ strengthening me. I am what I am by His free grace alone. *Not unto me, but unto Thy name, O Lord, alone be all the glory.*

Monday afternoon I preached to a great multitude at the parish church of St. Philip and Jacob. Thousands went away because there was no room for them within and God enabled me to read prayers and preach with great boldness.

Don't you opposers see how you do not prevail at all? Why do you not believe that it would not be this way unless God was with me? *Lord, open their eyes that they may see that this is your doing.*

About six in the evening I went to a new society. This, too, was crowded. Even though I had exerted myself so much at St. Philip's, I was enabled to expound with great freedom of spirit for above an hour. Then I went and spoke for nearly two hours to another society in Baldwin Street. Much power from above was among us. This done, I returned home full of joy, conversing, singing, and praying with many Christian brethren. We parted, rejoicing that God caused us to go on conquering.

"You Preach False Doctrine"

About ten the next morning, I visited the Reverend Chancellor of Bristol, who now plainly told me he intended to stop me. "I have sent for the registrar, sir," he stated, "to take down your answers." He then asked me by what authority I preached in the diocese of Bristol without a license.

I answered that I thought that custom had grown obsolete. "And why, pray, sir," I replied, "did you not ask this question of the Irish clergyman who preached for you last Thursday?"

"That was nothing to me," he answered. Then he read over part of the Ordination Office and those Canons that forbid any minister to preach in a private house, etc., and then asked me how I would reply to them.

"I understood those Canons did not belong to professed ministers of the Church of England," I answered.

"But," he returned, "they do."

"There is also a Canon," I remarked, "forbidding all clergymen to frequent taverns and play at cards. Why is that not enforced?"

"If somebody would complain of them," he returned, "then it would."

When I asked him why I was being given particular notice of my printed discourse, he said, "You preach false doctrine."

"Notwithstanding those Canons," I told him, "I could not but speak the things that I know. I am resolved to proceed as usual."

"Observe his answer, Mr. Registrar," he said. Turning to me he added, "I am resolved, sir, if you preach or expound anywhere in this diocese without a license, to first suspend and then excommunicate you."

I then turned to leave. He very civilly walked me to the door and told me that what he did was in the name of the clergy and laity of the city of Bristol. On my return home I found I had not so much joy as peace. I did not perceive the least resentment to arise in my heart. To show how little I regarded such threats, after I had joined in prayer for the chancellor, I immediately went to preach the Word at Newgate as usual. God gave me great joy again and wondrously pricked many to the heart.

At four I was expected to preach at St. Nicholas. Thousands went to hear me, but the lecturer sent word that orders were given that I could not preach in his church. *Lord, why do you so honor me?*

"Unspeakable Joy and Power"

At five, I went and expounded on James 1 to a Christian assembly who were much affected. Afterward I hastened to Nicholas Street, where a great crowd was waiting for me on the stairs, yard, and entry of the house, besides the room itself. I expounded on John 9 and exhorted all to imitate the poor beggar and not to fear men. God was pleased to fill me with unspeakable joy and power. All were wondrously touched. After my exposition, I prayed particularly for the chancellor. The whole company was in tears and said most earnest amens to all the petitions I put up for him. It is remarkable: we have not had such a continued presence of God among us since I was threatened to be excommunicated. But thus it was before, so it will be now. When we are cast out, Christ will more clearly reveal himself to us.

At three in the afternoon on Wednesday, according to my promise, I went to the coal miners at Kingswood. God highly favored us in sending a fine day, and nearly two thousand people were assembled on that occasion. I preached on John 3:3 for nearly an hour. God grant that the seed sown may fall on good ground, not stony or thorny.

About six in the evening I spoke to a society outside Lawford's Gate and afterward to another in Baldwin Street. Both were exceedingly crowded and attentive. At first I could not speak so strongly because I had exerted myself so much upon the mount. Afterward God gave me a fresh supply of grace and I was enabled to go through my work cheerfully. "Lo, I am with you alway, even unto the end of the world."

On Friday, February 23, at eleven, I went as usual and preached a written sermon at Newgate. After dinner I was taken very ill, so that I was obliged to lie upon the bed. Looking upon it as a thorn in the flesh, I went at three and preached to nearly four or five thousand people from a mount in Kingswood. The sun shone bright and people standing in such an awesome manner around the mount in the profoundest silence filled me with a holy admiration. *Lord, send forth more laborers into your harvest.*

This done, God strengthened me to expound to a society outside Lawford's Gate and afterward to two more in the city. I spoke with more freedom the last time than at the first. "When I am weak, then am I strong."

Boldness of Speech

About ten the next morning, I again visited the chancellor and showed him a letter I had received from the Lord Bishop of Bristol. My Lord gave me great boldness of speech and I asked the chancellor why he did not write to the bishop according to his promise. He answered he was to blame. I then insisted on his proving that I had preached false doctrine and reminded him of his threat to excommunicate me in the name of the clergy and laity of the city of Bristol. But he would have me think that he had said no such thing. He confessed at this time that he had neither heard me preach nor read any of my writings. I asked him his reasons for prohibiting my collecting for the Georgia Orphan House. He answered, "It would hinder the people's benefactions to the Bristol clergy."

"It would by no means hinder their contributions, and the clergy ought first to subscribe themselves, for example's sake," I replied.

After much conversation on this subject, I meekly told him I was resolved to go on preaching. If collections were not made here for the poor Georgians, I would lay it entirely upon him, adding that I would not be the one who should hinder such a design for the universe.

After I left the chancellor, I went and preached at Newgate. At three in the afternoon I went to a poorhouse outside Lawford's Gate, but the room and yard being full, I stood upon the steps going up to the house and preached to the crowd from there. Many who were passing along the road on horseback stood still to hear me. I hope many were bettered by what was spoken.

Sunday, at four, I hastened to Kingswood. There were about ten thousand people to hear me. The trees and hedges were full. All was hushed when I began. The sun shone bright and God enabled me to preach for an hour with great power—so loudly that all, I was told, could hear me. The fire is kindled in the country, and I know that all the devils in hell shall not be able to quench it.

On Sunday, March 4, I went to Newgate and preached with power to an exceedingly large congregation. I then hastened to Hannam Mount, three miles from the city, where the coal miners all live. God favored us with good weather. Over four thousand were ready to hear me, and God enabled me to preach with the demonstration of the Spirit. The ground not being high enough, I stood on a table. The sight of the people covering the green fields and paying deep attention pleased me much. I hope our Lord will feed all their souls with that bread which comes down from heaven, for many came from afar.

At four in the afternoon, I went to the mount on Rose Green and preached to over fourteen thousand. So good was my God that all could hear. I think it was worthwhile to come many miles to see such a sight. I spoke with great freedom, but thought all the while (as I do continually) that hereafter I shall suffer, as well as speak, for my Master's sake. *Lord, strengthen me against that hour.*

In the evening I expounded at Baldwin Street Society. I could not get up to the room without the utmost difficulty, the entry and court being so crowded. Blessed be God! The number of hearers much increases and, as my day is, so is my strength. This has been a sabbath indeed to my soul!

Banning the New Birth

I went to Bath with seven friends on March 12 and had the comfort of meeting there with some true followers of Jesus

Christ. I received news of the wonderful progress of the Gospel in Yorkshire under the ministry of Benjamin Ingham. I heard the mayor and sheriffs of Bristol had absolutely forbidden the warden of Newgate to let me preach there any longer because I insisted on the necessity of the new birth. The warden was much concerned and told them that I preached according to Scripture. But they were offended at him. "They answered and said unto him, Thou wast altogether born in sins, and dost thou teach us?"

Being forbidden to preach in the prison and being resolved not to give in to my adversaries, I preached to three or four thousand people at Baptist Mills, a place very near the city. My theme was "What think you of Christ?" Blessed be God! All things happen for the furtherance of the Gospel. I now preach to ten times more people than I would if I had been confined to the churches. Surely the devil and his emissaries are blind, or otherwise they would not thus confound themselves. Every day I am invited to new places. I will, by God's assistance, go to as many as I can. The rest I must leave unvisited till it shall please God to bring me back again from Georgia.

On Sunday the nineteenth, I was ill for about two hours, but was enabled to go and preach at Hannam to many more than were there last Sunday. In the afternoon, I really believe no less than twenty thousand were present at Rose Green. Blessed are the eyes which see the things we see. Surely God is truly with us. To behold such crowds standing about us in awesome silence and to hear the echo of their singing run from one end of them to the other is very solemn and surprising. My discourse continued for nearly an hour and a half. It pleased me to see with what cheerfulness the coal miners and other poor people threw in their mites.

Though I had a cold and did not feel well, God enabled me afterward to expound freely for more than an hour to a crowded society. I came home full of peace and joy in the Holy Spirit. What a mystery the divine life is! Oh, that all were partakers of it!

At Bath the next day, when dinner ended, through great weakness of body and sickness in my stomach, I was obliged to lie down upon the bed. When the hour came for my preaching, I went, weak and languid as I was, depending on divine strength. I don't think I ever preached with greater power. There were about four or five thousand, rich and poor, to hear me. I observed many scoffers, and when I stood on the table to preach, many laughed; but before I had finished my prayer, all was hushed and silent. Before I had concluded my discourse, God, by His Word, seemed to impress a great awe upon their minds. All were deeply attentive and seemed much affected with what had been spoken. Men may scoff for a little while, but there is something in this foolishness of preaching that will make the most stubborn heart to bend or break. "Is not my word like as a fire? saith the Lord; and like a hammer that breaketh the rock in pieces?"

Preaching to the Thousands

At Keynsham, in late March, I dined with an eminent Quaker in Bath. He entertained me and my friends in a most Christian manner. About three we left Bath, and though it was a wet day, we were gratefully surprised by meeting large numbers of horsemen from Bristol, besides several thousands from the neighboring villages, who came to hear me. Since I was refused to preach in the church, I did so on a mount. Our Master being with us, I preached with power. We came on our way rejoicing and reached Bristol about seven at night. I went immediately to Baldwin Street Society, and spoke on John 7. We also gave thanks for the great things we had seen and heard since we had met together last.

God will work and who shall hinder? I am shut out of the prison and my sister's house is not large enough to contain a fourth part of the people who come to me on a Sunday morning. God put it into the hearts of some gentlemen to lend me a large bowling green. There I preached to about five thousand people, and made a collection for my poor orphans till my hands were quite weary. Blessed be God that the bowling green is turned into a preaching place! This, I hope, is a token that assembly rooms and theaters will soon be put to the same use. Oh, may the Word of God be mighty to the pulling down of these strongholds of the devil!

About eight I went to the society in Nicholas Street. With great difficulty I at last reached the room, which was extremely hot. At the close of my exhortation, I recommended a charity school that was opened by the society today. I collected at the door myself, and few passed by without throwing in their mites.

Uncommonly Prepared in Prayer

At the bowling green, about four in the afternoon on Monday, I preached again to seven or eight thousand people. The sun shone brightly and the windows and balconies of the adjoining houses were filled with hearers. I was uncommonly prepared in prayer and carried out beyond myself in preaching, especially when I came to talk of the love and free grace of Jesus Christ. The people's concern was inexpressible. I am sure that thousands come not out of curiosity, but with a sincere desire of being fed with the milk of the Word. Afterward, I again collected for the Georgia Orphan House. It was nearly an hour and a half before the people could go out.

At eight I hastened to Weaver's Hall, in Temple Street, which was procured for me because the society rooms were too small. I was almost faint before I could get through the crowd, but God enabled me to speak with freedom. I believe there might have been a thousand hearers. Well may the devil and his servants rage horribly. Their kingdom is in danger.

One afternoon, after having been invited several times, I preached in a yard belonging to the Glass Houses. I was informed that many who dwell there neither fear God nor regard man. The audience numbered in the thousands. God enabled me to lay before them His threats and promises so that none need despair or presume. Oh, that I may be taught of God rightly to divide the Word of truth! While I was preaching, I heard many people behind me talking and making noise. I supposed they had been set on by somebody on purpose to disturb me. I was not in the least moved, but rather increased the more in strength. When I was done, I inquired the cause of that noise. I was informed that a man, being very drunk, had taken the liberty to call me "dog" and say that I ought to be horsewhipped. He offered money to any who would pelt me. Instead of that, the boys and people nearby began to cast stones and dirt at him. I expressed my dislike of their behavior, but could not help observing what sorry wages the devil gives his servants.

At the end of March, I preached one afternoon near Coal-Pit Hearth, seven miles from Bristol. I was earnestly invited there, where great numbers of coal miners live. I believe there were over two thousand people assembled on this occasion. The weather was exceedingly fair, and the hearers behaved very well. The place where I preached was near the maypole, so I took the opportunity to warn them of misspending their time in revelling and dancing. Oh, that all such entertainments were to stop! I see no other way to effect it but by going boldly and calling people from such lying vanities in the name of Jesus Christ. The reformation which is brought about by a coercive power will be only outward and superficial, but that which is done by the force of God's Word will be inward and lasting. *Lord, make me fit by grace for such a work, and then send me.*

Final Farewells

Saturday, March 31, at eleven, I went and gave the prisoners a farewell exhortation. I left orders concerning the distribution of the money that had been collected for them. At four, I preached as usual at the poorhouse where there was a larger assembly than ever. Almost nine pounds was gathered for the Georgia Orphan House. The longer I stay, the more my hearers increase. I was greatly refreshed with the sight of my honored friend, John Wesley, whom God's providence has sent to Bristol.

On Sunday, April 1, I preached at Bowling Green, Hannam, and Rose Green. At both places, the audience was much larger than before, especially at the latter. I was strengthened to cry aloud and to take my last farewell. As I was returning home, it comforted me exceedingly to hear almost everyone blessing me and wishing me a good voyage in the name of the Lord. My heart is so knit to the Bristol people that I could not leave them if I did not know John Wesley was left behind to teach them the way of God more perfectly. *Prosper, O Lord, the works of his hands upon him.*

Monday I spent a good part of the morning talking with those who came to say goodbye. Tongue cannot express what a sorrowful parting we had. Floods of tears flowed plentifully, and my heart was so melted that I prayed for them with cryings and many tears. About one, I was obliged to force myself away. Crowds were waiting at the door to give me a last farewell and nearly twenty friends accompanied me on horseback. Blessed be God for the marvelous great kindness He has shown me in this city. I believe many sinners have been effectually converted. Numbers have come to me under conviction, and all the children of God have been exceedingly encouraged. Various presents were sent me as tokens of their love. Several thousands of little books have been dispersed among the people, about two hundred pounds collected for the Georgia Orphan House, and many poor families relieved by the bounty of my friend Mr. Seward. What gives me the greater comfort is the consideration that my dear and honored friend, John Wesley, is there to confirm those who are awakened. When I return from Georgia, I hope to see many bold soldiers of Jesus Christ.

6

Charles Wesley: Seeking the Lost*

This morning, Friday, May 26, we joined in prayer for the poor prisoners while they went to execution, and at communion we commended their souls to Christ. The great comfort we found in this made us confidently hope that some of them were received as the penitent thief at the last hour. I dined with great liberty of spirit, being amazed to find my old enemy, intemperance, so suddenly subdued that I have almost forgotten I was ever in bondage to him. In the evening I broke through my own great unwillingness, and at last preached faith in Christ to an unexpected visitor.

On Saturday I felt a notion of anger from a trifling disappointment, but it was no sooner felt than conquered. I received communion, but still no sense of love, just comfort.

A gentlewoman, who has long been under the law, called to see me. Since she lived in the midst of opposers, I thought no good could be done by speaking, yet I was compelled to preach the Gospel. She seemed convinced and encouraged. After she had gone, I had much freedom to intercede for her and for another who continues to oppose the faith. Two or three other visitors were reproved of sin by the Holy Spirit of God. One

*Thomas Jackson, Ed., *op. cit.*, Vol. 1, pp. 98–120, May 26, 1738 through June 5, 1739.

seemed on the very border of Canaan, being fully convinced of righteousness and of Christ's imputed righteousness, while looking to receive it any moment by promise.

Trinity Sunday came and I rose in great heaviness, which neither private nor joint prayer could remove. At last I began intercession for my relatives, and was greatly helped by that, particularly by prayer for a most profligate sinner. I spent the morning in prayer and singing and rejoicing with a brother. In the afternoon John came. After a short prayer for success upon our ministry, we set out for Tiverton. I then began writing my first sermon in the name of Christ my Prophet.

Satan Under Her Feet

Today Mrs. Bray related to me the manner of her receiving faith in public prayers, and the great conflicts she has since had with Satan. For some days he so darkened the work of God that though her eye of faith had been opened to see herself encompassed with the blood of Christ, he still suggested to her that she did not believe because she did not have the joy that others had. She was being overpowered by his devices when in great heaviness she opened upon, "Lord, I believe: help thou my unbelief" (Mark 9:24). This helped her for a time, but the tempter still pursued—in the very words he had used to shake my brother's faith. She went to public prayers and prayed fervently. Toward the conclusion she saw Satan under her feet and came home in triumph of faith.

Gathering Sheep into the Fold

After dinner, other friends came. I thought some would now be gathered into the fold and was much encouraged to pray. I rose and saw a young lady under the work of God. I asked, urged, believed that she believed. She thought so too but was afraid to confess it. While she stood trembling and in tears, I opened the Bible and saw Isa. 30:18–19: "And therefore will the Lord wait, that he may be gracious unto you, and therefore will he be exalted, that he may have mercy upon you: for the Lord is a God of judgment: blessed are all they that wait for him. For the people shall dwell in Zion at Jerusalem; thou shalt weep no more: he will be very gracious unto thee at the voice of thy cry; when he shall hear it, he will answer thee."

She then opened the book of 2 Cor. 5:17: "Old things are passed away; behold, all things are become new." She read so far, and gave me the Bible to read on:

> "And all things are of God, who hath reconciled us to himself by Jesus Christ, and hath given to us the ministry of reconciliation; to wit, that God was in Christ, reconciling the world unto himself, not imputing their trespasses unto them; and hath committed unto us the word of reconciliation. Now then we are ambassadors for Christ, as though God did beseech you by us: we pray you in Christ's stead, be ye reconciled to God. For he hath made him to be sin for us, who knew no sin; that we might be made the righteousness of God in him." (2 Cor. 5:18–21)

Another then read: "Stand fast therefore in the liberty wherewith Christ hath made us free, and be not entangled again with the yoke of bondage" (Gal. 5:1). She now openly professed her faith and increased in confidence every moment. We joined in hearty thanks to God for His unspeakable gift. Just before parting, she opened the Bible to Luke 8:39: "Return to thine own house, and show how great things God hath done unto thee." This success was followed with inward trials, but at the same time I experienced the superior power of Christ.

Soon God enabled me, in spite of the devil and my own heart, to send a friend a simple account of what God had done for my soul.

A Cloud of Darkness

On Thursday, June 1, I was so troubled I could not pray, and was utterly dead at communion. Again on Friday I was still unable to pray, still dead in communion and full of a cowardly desire of death.

On Saturday my deadness continued, and the next day increased. I rose exceptionally heavy and averse to prayer so that I almost resolved not to go to church, which I had not been able to do till these two or three days past. When I did go, the prayers and communion were exceedingly grievous to me. I could not help asking myself the difference between what I am now and what I was before I believed.

I immediately answered that this darkness was not like the former darkness, because I was satisfied there was no guilt involved. I was assured it would be dispersed because, though I could not find I loved God or feel that He loved me, yet I did believe He loved me.

I returned home and lay down with the same load upon me. Even Benjamin Ingham's coming could not alleviate this. Others sang, but I had no heart to join—much less in public prayers. In the evening some others called. Though I was very averse to being with them, I forced myself to it, and spent two or three hours in singing, reading, and praying. This exercise revived me a little, and I found myself much helped toward prayer.

We prayed that if it was God's will, someone might now receive a word from Him. While I was yet speaking, Mr. Brown found power to believe. He rose and told me my prayer was heard and answered in Him. At the same time, John Burton opened the Bible to Col. 1:26–27: "Even the mystery which hath been hid from ages and from generations, but now is made manifest to his saints: to whom God would make known what is the riches of the glory of this mystery among the Gentiles; which is Christ in you, the hope of glory."

We were all full of joy and thanksgiving. Before we parted, I prayed with Mr. Brown and praised God for the great confirmation of my faith. The weight was quite taken off. I found power to pray with great earnestness, and rejoiced that my trials had continued so long in order to show me that when we are most cast down and most unable to help ourselves, it is then the best time of labor for our neighbor.

The Unspeakable Gift

I awakened on Monday thankful and with power to pray and praise. I had peace at communion and some attention in public prayer. In the afternoon I met John Burton at Islington. He told me God had given him faith while I was praying last night, but he thought it would do harm to declare it then. Upon finding his heart burn within him, he asked God to show him some token of his faith and immediately opened the Bible on Gen. 1:3: "Let there be light, and there was light." We rejoiced together in prayer and singing and left the rest of the company much stirred up to wait for the same unspeakable gift.

The next evening I read from Luther to a large company of our friends. John Burton was greatly affected. My inward temptations are, in a manner, uninterrupted. I never knew the energy of sin till I experienced the superior strength of Christ.

Wednesday morning I found myself under my Father's protection. While reading Matt. 7:7: "Ask, and it shall be given," I asked for some sense of His love in communion. It was there given me to believe assuredly that God loved me, even when I could have no sense of it. I had some imperfect perception of His love, and was strengthened to hope against hope after communion.

Defying the Tempter

Returning home in triumph, I found Dr. John Byrom. In defiance of the tempter, I simply told him the great things Jesus had done for me and many others. This brought on a full explanation of the doctrine of faith, which he received with wonderful readiness. Toward midnight I slept in peace.

At three, I took a coach for Blendon with Mr. Bray. During the ride I had a lengthy discussion with a lady passenger about the Fall and faith in Christ. She openly maintained the merit of good works. I wish all who oppose the righteousness of faith were so ingenious. They would then no longer seek it by the works of the law.

Before seven we came to Eltham. In riding on to Blendon, I was full of delight, seemingly in the new heavens. We prayed, sang, and shouted all the way.

Friday, while riding to Bexley with Henry Piers, I spoke of my experience in simplicity and confidence, and found him very ready to receive the faith. We spent the day in Bexley in the same manner, John Bray relating the inward workings of God upon his soul, and I the great things He had lately done for me and our friends at London. Henry listened eagerly to all that was said, not making the least objection, but confessing it was not something he had yet experienced. We walked, sang, and prayed in the garden. He was greatly moved, and testified his full conviction and desire of finding Christ. "But I must first," he said, "prepare myself my long exercise of prayer and good works."

The Skies Pour Down Righteousness

At night we joined in prayer for my sister Hetty. Never have I prayed with greater earnestness, expecting an immediate answer, and been so disappointed at not receiving it. I consulted the Scripture and met with Jesus' words to his men, "Let none go forth nor escape out of the city" (2 Kings 9:15). Then, "I trust in the Lord that I also myself shall come shortly" (Phil. 2:24). Still I was in great heaviness for her, and could not sleep till morning. Waking full of desire for her conversion, these words were brought to my remembrance, "The Spirit and the bride say, Come. And let him that heareth say, Come. And let him that is athirst come. And whosoever will, let him take the water of life freely" (Rev. 22:17). At this instant, a flash of lightning came, then thunder, then violent rain. I accepted it as a sign that the skies would soon pour down righteousness.

Yesterday we visited Miss Betsy. After the demon of secrecy was expelled from her she plainly informed me that after last receiving communion, she had heard a voice say, "Go thy way, thy sins are forgiven thee," which filled her with unspeakable joy. She said within herself, *Now I do indeed feed upon Christ in my heart by faith.* She thus continued all day in the spirit of triumph and exultation. All her life, she thought, would be too little to thank God for that day. But even after this, Satan got a great advantage over her, making her oppose the truth with fierceness. For many days she did not know that she had in herself a demonstration of the thing she denied. But after we had prayed that God would clear up His own work, the darkness dispersed. Those fears that her conversion was not real were all done away little by little.

Deathbed Grace

On Tuesday, June 13, Henry Piers was asked to visit a dying woman. She was in despair for having done so much evil and so little good. He declared to her the glad tidings of salvation, that all her good, were it ten thousand times more, could never save her. He also told her that all her evil could never hurt her if she would repent and believe, if she could lay hold on Christ by a living faith and look for salvation by grace alone. This was comfort indeed. She gladly gave up her own merits for Christ's, and the Holy Spirit wrought peace in her heart, which she expressed in a calm, cheerful, triumphant expectation of death. Her fears and agonies were at an end. Being justified by faith, she had peace with God. She only entered further into her rest when she died a few hours later. The spectators were melted into tears. She calmly passed into the heavenly Canaan, and has there brought up a good report of her faithful pastor, who, under Christ, saved her soul from death.

These were the firstfruits of Henry's ministry. I find him strengthened in this, and more assured that the Gospel is the power of God unto salvation, to every one who believes.

At London I was informed that my brother had gone with Benjamin Ingham to Germany. The news surprised but did not disquiet me.

On Wednesday, June 21, the Lord gave us more reason for

thanksgiving at Blendon, where I read my brother's sermon on faith. When it was over, the gardener declared faith had come to him by hearing it, and he had no doubt of his sins being forgiven. "Were I to die just now," he added, "I know I would be accepted through Christ Jesus."

Eleventh-Hour Faith

On Friday I accompanied Henry Piers on a visit to a poor old woman, whom he never could prevail upon to go to church. I expected we would be called to preach the Law, but found her ready for the Gospel and very happy to exchange her merits for Christ's.

The last of June I called upon Goody Dickenson and asked if she now had forgiveness. "Yes," she said, "I received it in the midst of your sermon."

"Do you then believe Christ died for you personally?"

"Yes, to be sure. I must believe it if I would not deny the Scripture." She expressed strong confidence in God, appeared full of love toward two beggars that called, believed she would be saved if she died now, and promised to come to church, even if only in rags. In short, she left me no reason to doubt that she was taken in at the eleventh hour, being now near sixty.

Later, William Delamotte told me he had written two pages against our truth, but in seeking after more texts, had met one that quite spoiled all: "Not by works of righteousness which we have done, but according to his mercy he saved us" (Titus 3:5). This convinced him, and immediately he burned all he had written. I asked what it was he still struck at.

"Nothing," he answered, "but God's giving faith instantaneously."

I replied that that alone hindered his receiving it just now. No more preparation is necessary to receive faith than what God is pleased to give.

Laying Hold of the Promises

We went to prayers, pleading the promises for William. While we were praying, and singing, and reading, alternately, a poor illiterate carpenter, Mr. Heather, came to talk with me. He had heard and liked the sermon upon faith. I asked him whether he had faith. He said, "No." I asked if he had forgiveness of sins. "No," he uttered. I asked whether there was or could be any good in him till he believed. "No," he concluded.

"But do you think Christ cannot give you faith and forgiveness in this hour?"

"Yes, to be sure He can."

"And do you believe His promise that when two of His disciples shall agree upon earth, as touching anything they shall ask of Him, He will give it to them?"

"I do."

"Why, then, here is your minister, and I agree to ask faith for you."

"Then I believe I shall receive it before I go out of the room."

We went to prayer and pleaded the promise. Upon rising, I asked him whether he believed.

His answer was, "Yes, I do believe with all my heart. I believe Christ died for my sins. I know they are all forgiven. I desire only to love Him. I would suffer anything for Him and could lay down my life for Him this moment."

I turned to William and asked, "Do you now believe that God can give faith instantaneously?" He was too full to speak, but told me afterward he envied the unopposing ignorance and simplicity of the poor, and wished himself that illiterate carpenter.

Next day I returned to town, rejoicing that God had added to His living church seven more souls through my ministry.

"Whole from That Hour"

I went to Peter Sims' in expectation of a moving of the Holy Spirit. Several of our friends were providentially brought there.

We joined in singing and prayer. The last time we prayed, I could not stop but was forced to go on. I rose at last and saw William Chapman still kneeling. I opened the book and read aloud, "And, behold, a woman, which was diseased with an issue of blood twelve years, came behind him, and touched the hem of his garment: for she said within herself, If I may but touch his garment, I shall be whole. But Jesus turned him about, and when he saw her, he said, Daughter, be of good comfort; thy faith hath made thee whole. And the woman was made whole from that hour" (Matt. 9:20–22).

My heart burned within me while I was reading. At the same time I heard him cry out with great struggling, "I do believe."

We lifted him up, for he had not power to rise of himself, being quite helpless, exhausted, and in a profuse sweat. An old believer among us acknowledged himself affected with a wonderful sympathy. We had the satisfaction of seeing Mr. Chapman increase in faith, and returned most hearty thanks to the God of his and our salvation.

The first thing I felt the following day, thanks be to God, was a fear of pride and desire to love. Betsy Delamotte called and gave me the following letter:

Dear Sir,

God has heard your prayers. Yesterday, about twelve, He put His sanction to the desires of his distressed servant, and glory be to Him, I have enjoyed the fruits of His Holy Spirit ever since. The only uneasiness I feel is lack of thankfulness and love for so unspeakable a gift. But I am confident of this also, that the same gracious hand which has communicated will communicate even unto the end.

I am your sincere friend in Christ,
William Delamotte

In reading this, I felt true thankfulness, and was quite melted down with God's goodness to my friend.

Faith Obscured by Worldly Cares

Saturday, July 1, I was again at Mrs. Claggett's. The eldest daughter and Mrs. Claggett joined us. I related the cure of the lame girl at Bath. She rejoiced to hear that a person might have faith and have it long obscured by worldly cares, yet not lost. She said the maid's case was hers. She now professed faith and said the darkness she had long lain under was a just punishment for her not giving God the glory. We sang and rejoiced together—then went to the house of God as friends. In the lesson, God related His past kindness to her. "And he was teaching in one of the synagogues on the sabbath. And, behold, there was a woman which had a spirit of infirmity eighteen years, and was bowed together, and could in no wise lift up herself. And when Jesus saw her, he called her to him, and said unto her, Woman, thou art loosed from thine infirmity. And he laid his hands on her: and immediately she was made straight, and glorified God" (Luke 13:10–13). Mrs. Claggett was deeply affected, and told me afterward that her not following the woman's example of glorifying God had occasioned all the troubles in her life. She was now resolved, as far as possible to repair her past unfaithfulness.

At Mr. Sims' I was extremely averse to prayer and would have stolen away without it, but Mr. Bray stopped me, saying my deadness could not hinder God, and forced me to pray. I had scarcely begun when I was quite melted down and prayed more fervently than ever before. A poor man who came in at the beginning of the prayer confessed his faith before us all, being full of joy and triumph. He had never found himself like this before. He knew his sins were forgiven and could gladly die that moment.

Forgiven and Overpowered with His Love

Being selected to preach Sunday morning, July 2, for the first time, I received strength for the work of the ministry in prayer and singing. The whole service at Basingshaw was wonderfully animating, especially the parable concerning the miraculous catch of fishes. I preached salvation by faith to a very attentive audience and then communion. Observing a woman deeply reverent, I asked her if she had forgiveness of sins. She answered with great sweetness and humility, "Yes, I know it now. I have forgiveness."

I preached again at London Wall without fear or weariness. As I was going into the church, a woman caught hold of my hand and blessed me most heartily, telling me she had received forgiveness of sins while I was preaching in the morning.

In the evening, a group of us met at Peter Sims'. There was a Mrs. Harper there who had that day received the Spirit by the hearing of faith but was afraid to confess it. We sang a hymn to Christ. At the words, "Who for me, for me hath died," she burst into tears and cried, "I believe! I believe!" and sank down. As she continued to confess, she increased in the assurance of faith, full of peace, joy, and love.

We sang and prayed again. I observed one of the maids running out. I followed and found her full of tears, joy, and love. I asked what ailed her. She answered as soon as joy would let her, that Christ died for her! She appeared quite overpowered with His love.

Every Soul on Deathrow

On Monday, July 10, at Mr. Sparks' request, I went with him, John Bray, and John Burnham to Newgate. I preached with a heavy heart to ten prisoners under sentence of death. My old prejudice against deathbed repentance still hung upon me. I could hardly hope there was mercy for those whose time was so short. But in the midst of my weak sermon, a sudden spirit of faith came upon us. I promised them all pardon in the name of Jesus Christ if they would then, as at the last hour, repent and believe the Gospel. I believed they would accept His mercy, and could not help telling them I had no doubt but that

God would receive every one of them.

The next day, taking my sermon from the second lesson, I preached with earnestness to the prisoners. One or two of them were deeply affected. Then on Wednesday, I again preached at Newgate to the condemned felons, and hearing of one sick of a fever I visited him in his cell. He was a poor black who had robbed his master. I told him of One who came down from heaven to save lost sinners, him in particular. I described the sufferings of the Son of God, His sorrows, agony, and death. He listened with all the signs of eager astonishment, and tears trickled down his cheeks while he cried, "What! Was it for me? Did God suffer all this for so poor a creature as me?"

I left him waiting for the salvation of God.

Thursday I again read prayers and preached at Newgate, and administered communion to our friends, with five of the felons. I was much affected and assisted in prayer for them, exhorting them with great comfort and confidence.

On Friday I spoke strongly to the poor prisoners and to the sick black man in the condemned hole, moved by his sorrow and earnest desire for Christ Jesus.

Saturday I preached there again with an encouraged heart, and rejoiced with my poor happy black who now believed the Son of God loved him and gave himself for him.

Monday, July 17, I rose and preached on death at Newgate, which they must suffer the day after tomorrow. Mr. Sparks assisted in giving communion. At one, I was with the black man in his cell, James Hutton assisting. Two more of the prisoners came. I had great help and power in prayer. One rose and said he felt his heart all on fire as never before. He believed Christ died for him. I found myself overwhelmed with the love of Christ to sinners. The black man was quite happy. The other criminal was in an excellent frame of mind, believing, or on the point of it. I talked with another concerning faith in Christ and he was greatly moved. The Lord, I trust, will help his unbelief also.

At six, I took Bray and Fish to Newgate again, and talked

chiefly with Hudson and Newington. Newington declared he had felt inexpressible joy and love some time ago in prayer, but was much troubled at its being so soon withdrawn. The Lord gave us power to pray, and they were deeply affected. We have great hopes for both of them.

Tuesday, July 18, the chaplain read prayers and preached. I administered communion to the black man and eight more, having first instructed them in the nature of it. I spoke comfortably to them afterward.

In the cells, one told me that whenever he attempted to pray, or had a serious thought, something came along and hindered him. After we had prayer for him in faith, he rose amazingly comforted, full of joy and love, so that we could not doubt his having received salvation.

Locked into Joy on Deathrow

At night I was locked in with Bray in one of the cells. We wrestled in mighty prayer. All the criminals were present, and all delightfully cheerful. The guard, in particular, found his comfort and joy increase every moment. One prisoner, from the time he had communion, had been in perfect peace. Joy was visible in all their faces. We sang:

"Behold the Savior of mankind,
    Nailed to the shameful tree!
How vast the love that Him inclined
    To bleed and die for thee . . . ."

It was one of the most triumphant hours I have ever known.

Yet on Wednesday, I rose very heavy as I prepared to visit them for the last time. At six I prayed and sang with them all together. The chaplain would read prayers and preach most miserably. Mr. Sparks and Thomas Broughton were present. I felt my heart full of tender love to the latter. He administered communion, and all ten received. Then he prayed, and I after him.

At half-past nine, their irons were knocked off, and their

hands tied. I went in a coach with Sparks, Washington, and a friend of Newington. By half-past ten we came to Tyburn, waited till eleven, then these men appointed to die were brought to us. I got up on the cart with Sparks and Broughton. The chaplain endeavored to follow, but the poor prisoners begged that he not come, and the mob kept him down.

Impatient to Be with Jesus

I prayed first, and then Sparks and Broughton prayed. We had prayed before that our Lord would show there was a power superior to the fear of death. Newington had quite forgotten his pain. The prisoners were all full of comfort, peace, and triumph. They knew Christ waited to receive them into paradise because I had assured them that He had died for them. Greenaway was impatient to be with Jesus.

The black man spied me coming out of the coach and saluted me with his looks. As often as his eyes met mine, he smiled with the most composed, delightful countenance I had ever seen. Read caught hold of my hand in a transport of joy. Newington seemed perfectly pleased. Hudson declared he was never better or more at ease in mind and body. None showed any natural terror of death, no crying or tears. All expressed their desire that we follow them to paradise. I never saw such calm triumph, such incredible indifference to dying. We sang several hymns particularly,

"Behold the Savior of mankind,
   Nailed to the shameful tree,"

and the hymn entitled "Faith in Christ" which concludes,

"A guilty, weak, and helpless worm,
   Into Thy hands I fall,
Be Thou my life, my righteousness,
   My Jesus, and my all."

In earnest faith, we asked Jesus to receive their spirits. I could do nothing but rejoice as I kissed Newington and Hudson, and then took leave of each in particular. Thomas Broughton told them not to be surprised when the cart drew away. They cheerfully replied they would not, but expressed some concern as to how we would get back to our coach. We left them going to meet their Lord, ready for the Bridegroom.

When the cart drew off, no one stirred or struggled for life, but meekly gave up their spirits. They were cut down exactly at twelve. I spoke a few suitable words to the crowd and returned, full of peace and confidence in our friends' happiness. That hour under the gallows was the most blessed hour of my life.

Reproached for the Gospel

In the coach to London, in late July, I preached faith in Christ. A lady passenger was extremely offended and claimed in plain terms her own good works. She asked if I was a Methodist and threatened to beat me. I declared I deserved nothing but hell, and so did she, and she must confess it before she could have a title to heaven. This was most intolerable to her. The other passengers were less offended and began to listen. They asked where I preached. A maid servant devoured every word.

On Saturday, August 12, we were warmed by reading George Whitefield's published journal. As I walked with Charles Metcalf and others in great joy, wishing for a place in which to sing, a blacksmith stopped us. We turned into his house, sang a hymn, and went on our way rejoicing.

Sunday I preached at Islington, and gave communion to a sick woman who was therein assured of her reconciliation to God through Christ Jesus. On Tuesday I served communion again to the sick woman. Mrs. Claggett and her daughters made up the greater part of the congregation. We were all comforted. I seldom fail seeing them and Islington once a day.

Wednesday I was dragged out by Mr. Bray to Jepheniah Harris's religious society. There, after much disputing, I confuted, rather than convinced, them by reading the homily on justification.

The next Thursday I preached faith to a dying woman and then administered communion. She was satisfied God had sent us and told me I was the instrument of saving her soul.

"Had you then no faith before we came?" I asked.

"No. How should I? It is the gift of God, and He never gave it to me till now," she answered.

"Do you now think you shall be saved?"

"Yes," she replied, smiling. "I have no doubt of it."

"You need not then fear the devil's hurting you."

"I know that. He is chained. I have nothing to do with him, or he with me."

She promised to carry a good report of us to those she was going to. A young man also received faith in that hour.

Sunday, September 10, I preached faith in the morning at Sir George Wheler's chapel and assisted at communion. In the afternoon I preached at St. Botolph's. In the evening at Sims', I was much strengthened to pray and expound to more than three hundred attentive souls. Another lost sheep was now brought home. Believers and seekers increase in number.

On Saturday, September 16, James Hutton came and took me to Newgate, where we preached Christ to four condemned prisoners. That night John returned from Germany. We took counsel together, comparing our experiences.

Then on Sunday, at the early communion, John read prayers. I preached in Gracechurch Street in the morning, and at Queen's Street Chapel in the afternoon, exhorting that all are under sin and in need of salvation. In the evening I preached at the Savoy Society, bringing a message on faith, from Romans 3. John entertained us with his Moravian experiences.

He Remains True to His Promise

Late in October, few were present at St. Antholin's, so I thought of preaching extemporaneously. I was afraid, yet ventured on the promise, "Lo, I am with you alway" (Matt. 28:20). I spoke on justification, from Romans 1, for three-quarters of an hour without hesitation. Glory be to God, who keeps His promises forever.

On a November Thursday, after morning prayers, I baptized Mrs. Bell. I sang and prayed with assistance at Mr. Stonehouse's. Then Mrs. Wren confessed she had been in bondage ten years, but received salvation on Tuesday night while we were praying. She was now perfectly free, full of peace and joy in believing. Another lady professed her faith in recently receiving Christ.

Mrs. Hankinson took me to a poor woman. She was broken, bruised, and bound by sin. After prayer she arose, loosed from her bondage, and glorified God.

Saturday, November 18, I had a joyful meeting with my dear Charles Delamotte, who had just returned from Georgia. He said he had received forgiveness five months ago, and continued in peace and liberty.

Sunday I preached in Dr. Crow's church at Bishopsgate. Later I visited a poor woman of eighty-four, who told me she was assured of salvation because of some work she had done for God. She was soon shown her own works would not save her and in the midst of prayer she was set at liberty. She rose, caught hold of me, and declared her salvation. She was now at ease and ready to go into eternity. She prayed for and blessed me.

Rooming with the Devil

Monday, December 11, I took the coach to Wycombe. I lodged at Mr. Hollis's, who told me about his French prophets who were equal, in his account, if not superior, to the Old Testament ones. While we were talking, he fell into violent agitations and gobbled like a turkey cock. I was frightened and began exorcising him with, "Thou deaf and dumb devil," and so on. He soon recovered. I prayed and went to bed, though I did not sleep very soundly with Satan so near me. I got to London by one the next day. George Whitefield came to John Bray's soon after I arrived, and I heard him preach to a vast throng at St. Helen's. Late in December I went to preach at St. Antholin's. The clerk asked me my name and then said, "Dr. Venn has forbidden any Methodist to speak. Do you call yourself a Methodist?" "I do not. The world may call me what it pleases."

"Well, sir," he said, "It is a pity the people should go away without preaching. You may preach."

So I preached on good works.

On December 26, George Whitefield preached. We had communion on this and the four following days. On Thursday John preached; on Friday, George; and on Saturday, Mr. Robson. The whole week was a festival indeed, a joyful season, holy unto the Lord.

Freed from the Devil's Power

On Thursday, January 25, when I expounded at Brockmar's, the Lord's presence was very evident. As I was leaving, a woman stopped me from departing and confessed that she was under the power of the devil. Then she fell at my feet. We prayed in confidence and, on my mentioning in prayer the forgiven adultress, she cried out, "I have received the comfort!" I was filled with love, joy, and triumph.

During February I preached at the Marshalsea jail. I was sent for by a dying harlot, and preached Christ the friend of sinners. I trust it reached her heart. After I read prayers at Islington, Miss Crisp invited me to her home. I prayed for her with great earnestness. Later, at the society, I expounded on the woman of Samaria. When I had finished, she ran to me and cried, "I do, I do believe! These words you spoke came with power, 'Him that cometh to me I will in no wise cast out' (John 6:37). An unknown peace flowed with them into my soul." We sang, rejoiced, and gave thanks to the pardoning God in her behalf.

In Quest of Lost Sheep

Sunday, February 18, I preached at Islington, on the woman that was a sinner, and at Marshalsea, from Romans 3. I prayed with a sick harlot.

A few days later I prayed in the prison with Ann Dodd, who was weary of sin and longed to break loose. I preached powerfully about Judgment Day. Then I prayed to God for the poor harlots. Our sisters took one away in triumph. I followed to Mrs. Hanson's, who took charge of that returning prodigal. Our hearts were overflowing with pity for her. She seemed confounded and silent, testifying her joy and love only by her tears. We sang and prayed over her in great confidence.

The next day I waked full of concern for the poor harlot and began singing a hymn for her. At five I expounded on the woman taken in adultery.

The following day I went in quest of the lost sheep and found her coming with John Bray from public prayer. She had been in deep distress, pierced with every word at the last two services. She almost fainted this morning, weary and heavy-laden. She told Bray God could not forgive her because her sins were so great. She could not bear our triumph. We wrestled in prayer for her, and she declared her burden lifted and her soul at peace. The more we prayed, the clearer she was, until at last she testified that she believed in Jesus with her whole heart. We continued in mighty prayer for all gross sinners, and I offered myself willingly to be employed particularly in their service.

Justification by Faith Causes Walkout

On Sunday, February 25, I preached justification by faith at Bexley. In the beginning of my discourse about twenty left the church. They were more pleased, or at least more patient in the afternoon, when I preached on the woman at our Savior's feet. Later at Blendon I was faint and spent, but I was revived by exhorting almost two hundred of the poor.

The next Saturday I expounded to some three hundred hearers at Beech Lane. The Saturday after, I went to Newgate with my usual reluctance, but preached with freedom. In prayer I had great power, as all present seemed to confess.

On Monday I was again at Newgate with Bray. I prayed, sang, and exhorted with great life and vehemence. I talked in the cells to two Catholics who renounced all merit but that of Jesus Christ. Later I expounded at Bray's on Judgment Day. The power of the Lord was present and working. A woman cried out as if in agony. Another sank down overpowered. All were moved and melted as wax before a fire. At eight I expounded on Dowgate Hill, where two more were taken into the fold by the Holy Spirit.

"That's a Lie!"

When expounding at Mr. Crouch's on persecution, a man cried out, "That's a lie!" We began to pray and sing. The power of Jesus was in the midst of us, and the man became quite docile. Another asked what comfort and joy meant. I calmly invited him to experience it.

On Wednesday, March 28, we attempted to dissuade my brother John from going to Bristol because of an unaccountable fear that it would prove fatal to him. A great power was among us. John offered himself willingly to whatever the Lord would appoint. The next day he set out, commended by us to the grace of God. He left a blessing behind, but I desired to die with him.

Sunday, April 1, as I prayed at Fetter Lane that the Lord might be in the midst of us, I received a remarkable answer. A man by the name of Nowers had strong pangs, groaned, screamed, and roared out. I was neither offended nor edified by it. We sang and praised God with all our might. I did not get home till eleven.

The following Friday I convinced a woman of sin, and found another convinced of righteousness. A man who had rejected me was also overpowered by the Holy Spirit.

On Sunday evening, April 15, we found prayers answered at the society meeting. Two received forgiveness and many were filled with unutterable groanings. All received some spiritual gift. We could not part, and continued our triumph all night long.

The last of April, I heard George Whitefield preach in Islington churchyard. The large congregation could not have been more affected even if they had been within the church walls.

Forbidden to Preach

On Sunday, at the Islington vestry meeting, the churchwardens forbade my preaching and demanded my local license. I said nothing but that I heard them. They were very abusive and said, "You all have the spirit of the devil," mentioning Whitefield, Stonehouse, and me by name.

After prayers, George Stonehouse opened a way for me to the pulpit. I offered to go up when a Mr. Cotteril forcibly kept me back. I thought, "The servant of the Lord must not strive" (2 Tim. 2:24) and yielded. Mr. Streat preached and I assisted at communion. Afterward, I preached at our house, and prayed fervently for the opposers. I waited for Justice Elliot, who had gone into the vestry and severely chided the churchwardens who had made the clerk read the canon and call the vestry meeting. Mr. Streat asked Stonehouse to stop me from ever preaching there again. Later, I heard that George had had over ten thousand hearers for his preaching that day.

The first Tuesday in May, at Islington, during the time of prayers, the churchwardens still kept guard on the pulpit stairs so I could not preach. I was not inclined to fight my way through them. George Stonehouse preached a thundering sermon to sear their consciences. A poor harlot was struck down by the word. She, and all others, were melted into tears. Prayers and strong cries went up for her. I have a good hope his brand will also be plucked out of the fire. On Wednesday she came to the

Fetter Lane meeting where I expounded on the prodigal. In mid-May I accompanied George Whitefield to Blackheath. He preached in the rain to many listening sinners. In the evening at Fetter Lane a dispute arose about lay preaching. Many, particularly John Bray and William Fish, were very much in favor of it. George Whitefield and I declared against it.

Saturday, May 19, at the common, George preached from Acts 1:18: "The Holy Ghost is come upon you." He estimated about five thousand attended.

At noon on Friday, May 25, I set out on horseback, our sisters in the coach. By two the next day, we surprised Miss Betty at Broadoaks. I was full of prayer that the Lord would gather a church in this place.

The New Birth Opposed

Wyseman Claggett is still opposed to my preaching. I went to church, where I preached on the new birth. It was such a wonderful meeting that we returned singing. But Claggett was still more violent, so I told him he was doing the devil's work. Between jest and earnest, he struck me and raged exceedingly at seeing the people come flocking to hear the Word. However, God gave me utterance to preach the Gospel to four or five hundred there.

On Tuesday, a farmer by the name of Franklyn invited me to preach in his field. I did so expounding on, "Repent: for the kingdom of heaven is at hand" (Matt. 4:17), to about five hundred and returned home rejoicing.

The next day I convinced a sick man of unbelief. Another on his deathbed received forgiveness and witnessed a good confession. I invited nearly a thousand sinners, weary and heavy-laden, who filled the whole house at night, to come to Christ for rest.

On Thursday, May 31, a Quaker sent me a preaching invitation to preach at Thackstead. I objected to preaching in another's parish till I had been refused the church. Many Quakers and nearly seven hundred others attended, while I declared in the highways, "The Scripture has included all under sin."

On Friday I preached to more than one thousand attentive sinners on Matt. 1:21: "He shall save his people from their sins." Many showed their emotion by tears.

The following Sunday, George Whitefield preached in the morning in Moorfield's and in the evening at Kennington Common. That day there were more than had ever attended. The next day I walked with a young Quaker to Islington church, where Mr. Scott baptized him.

He told me afterward, "When the words were speaking, I felt the Holy Spirit descend into my soul. My joy rose higher and higher till at last I could neither speak nor move, but seemed rapt into the third heaven."

In June I stood by George Whitefield while he preached on the mount in Blackheath. The crowd was nearly as large as at Kennington. The cries of the wounded were heard on every side. "What has Satan gained by turning him out of the churches?" they asked.

Part 3

The Vicious Opposition to Revival

7

*John Wesley: Confronting the Devil**

This morning, there were many who came to me, earnestly urging me not to preach in the afternoon because several people had threatened to do terrible things to me. Because this report was spread around, many of the "better sort of people" came to see the threats fulfilled. I believe this added more than a thousand to the ordinary congregation. The scripture (Isa. 41:10) was not my choice, but given by the providence of God. It directed me, "Fear thou not; for I am with thee: be not dismayed; for I am thy God. I will strengthen thee; yea, I will help thee; yea, I will uphold thee with the right hand of my righteousness." The power of God came with this word, so that none scoffed, interrupted, or opened his mouth.

"By the Authority of Jesus Christ . . ."

The next day, at Bath, there was great expectation of what a noted man had threatened to do to me. I was much advised

*Nehemiah Curnock, *op. cit.*, pp. 74–89, May 29, 1738 through October 28, 1739.

not to preach, because no one knew what might happen. By this report I also gained a much larger audience, among whom were many of the rich and the great. I told them plainly, the Scripture had proved them all—high and low, rich and poor—to be under sin. Many of them seemed a little surprised, and while this was sinking in with seriousness, their champion appeared. Coming close to me, he asked by what authority I did these things.

I replied, "By the authority of Jesus Christ, conveyed to me by the Archbishop of Canterbury when he laid hands upon me and said, 'Take your authority to preach the Gospel.' "

"This is contrary to an Act of Parliament," he said. "This is an illegal religious assembly."

"Sir," I answered, "the assemblies mentioned in that Act, as the preamble shows, are seditious meetings. This is not such. There is no shadow of sedition here; therefore it is not contrary to the act."

"I say it is," he replied, "and besides, your preaching is frightening people out of their wits."

"Sir, did you ever hear me preach?"

"No."

"How then can you judge of what you never heard?"

"Sir, by common report."

"Common report is not enough. Permit me to ask, sir, is not your name Nash?"

"My name is Nash."

"Sir, I dare not judge of you by common report. I think it not enough to judge by."

Here he paused awhile, and having recovered himself, said, "I desire to know what these people come here for."

Hearing this, one replied, "Sir, leave him to me. Let an old woman answer him. You, Mr. Nash, take care of your body. We take care of our souls, and we come here for food for our souls."

Without a word he walked away.

As I returned, the street was full of people hurrying to and fro and speaking incessantly. But when any of them asked,

"Which is he?" and I replied, "I am he," they were immediately silent.

The Plain Truth

Several ladies followed me into Mr. Merchant's house where the servant told me there were some who wanted to speak to me. I went to them and said, "I believe, ladies, the maid is mistaken. You only wanted to look at me. I do not expect that the rich and great should want either to speak with me or to hear me, for I speak the plain truth. That is something you hear little of, and do not desire to hear." A few more words passed between us, and I left the room.

On Thursday I preached at Priest Down. In the midst of praying after the sermon, two men, hired for that purpose, began singing a ballad. After a few mild words, used without effect, we all began singing a psalm putting them utterly to silence. We then poured out our souls in prayer for the two men. From that time they were altogether confounded.

On Wednesday morning I came to London and had an opportunity to see my mother, whom I had not seen since my return from Germany. At six I warned the women at Fetter Lane Society, knowing how they had been recently disturbed, not to believe every spirit, but to try the spirits, whether they were of God. Our brethren met at eight, and it pleased God to remove many misunderstandings and offenses that had crept in among them.

Twelve Thousand Listen

Thursday, I went with George Whitefield to Blackheath, where there were twelve or fourteen thousand people. He surprised me by asking me to preach in his place. This I did, on my favorite subject, "Jesus Christ, who by God is made unto us wisdom, righteousness, sanctification and redemption."

I was greatly moved with compassion for the rich that were

there, to whom I made a particular application. Some of them seemed to listen, while others drove away in their coaches, not wanting to hear from such an uncouth preacher as I.

I talked at length with one who is called a Quaker, but he would not receive my ideas. I was too strict for him, he said, and talked of a perfection he did not think necessary. He was persuaded there was no harm in costly apparel, provided it was plain and grave, nor in putting scarlet or gold upon our houses as long as it was not upon our clothes.

Twenty-six Fall to the Ground

Friday evening I went to a society at Wapping, weary in body and faint in spirit. I intended to speak on Rom. 3:19, but knew not how to start. During our time of singing, my mind was searching for a scripture in the Epistle to the Hebrews. I begged God to direct, and opened the book to 10:19: "Having therefore, brethren, boldness to enter into the holiest by the blood of Jesus, by a new and living way."

After I had finished preaching and was earnestly inviting all sinners to enter into the holiest by this new and living way, many of those who had heard began to call upon God with strong cries and tears. Some sank down, having no strength remaining in them. Others trembled and quaked exceedingly. Some were torn with a kind of convulsive motion in every part of their bodies, often so violently that sometimes four or five persons could not hold one of them. I have seen many hysterical and many epileptic fits, but in most respects none of them were like these. I immediately prayed that God would not allow those who were weak to be offended.

However, one woman was greatly offended, being sure those so affected could stop the shaking if they wished. No one could persuade her to the contrary. She had gone only three or four yards when she also dropped down in as violent an agony as the rest. Twenty-six had been so affected. Most of them were filled with peace and joy during the prayers which were made for them. All promised to meet me the next day, but only eighteen came. By talking closely with them, I found reason to believe that some of them had gone home justified. The rest seemed to be waiting patiently for a manifestation of that experience with God.

On Saturday we met at Fetter Lane to humble ourselves before God. He had justly withdrawn His Spirit from us for our manifold unfaithfulness. Again we found God with us, as at the first. Some fell prostrate upon the ground under His power. Others burst out, as with a single mind, into loud praise and thanksgiving.

On Sunday I preached at seven in Upper Moorfields to six or seven thousand people. At five I preached on Kennington Common to about fifteen thousand people, on Isa. 45:22: "Look unto me, and be ye saved, all the ends of the earth."

Too Full of Love and Joy to Walk

I left London early Monday morning. The next evening I reached Bristol and preached to a large congregation. Howel Harris called on me an hour or two later. He said he had been much dissuaded from either hearing me or seeing me by many who said all manner of evil of me. "But as soon as I heard you preach," he stated, "I quickly found of what spirit you were. Before you were done, I was so overpowered with joy and love that I had much trouble walking home."

Sunday morning as I was riding to Rose Green in a smooth, plain part of the road, my horse suddenly lurched and fell on his head. She rolled over and over, yet I received no other hurt than a little bruise on one side, which at the time I didn't feel. I preached without pain to six or seven thousand people on 1 Cor. 10:31: "Whether therefore ye eat, or drink, or whatsoever ye do, do all to the glory of God."

About ten on Monday morning, a lady sitting at work was suddenly seized with severe terrors of mind and strong trembling. She continued in this all afternoon, but at the society meeting in the evening, God turned her heaviness into joy. Five or six others were also cut to the heart this day, as was one who had been mourning many months without any to comfort her. Jesus came to them all with His comfort.

The first Friday of July, in the afternoon, I recognized George Whitefield, who had just come from London, to Baptist Mills, where he preached concerning the Holy Spirit, which all who believe are to receive. We were given severe censure from those who preach as if there were no Holy Spirit.

Outward Signs of the Inward Work

On Saturday George Whitefield and I discussed outward signs which had so often accompanied the inward work of God. I found his objections were chiefly grounded on the gross misrepresentations he heard concerning these facts. The next day he had an opportunity of informing himself better, for no sooner had he begun to invite sinners to believe in Christ than four persons collapsed close to him. One of them lay without either sense or motion. A second trembled exceedingly. The third had strong convulsions over his entire body but made no noise other than groans. The fourth convulsed equally and called upon God with strong cries and tears. From this time, I trust we shall all allow God to carry on His own work in the way that pleases Him.

The next Friday afternoon, I left Bristol with George in the midst of heavy rain. The clouds soon dispersed so that we had a fair, calm evening, and a serious congregation gathered at Thornbury.

We had an attentive congregation at Gloucester in the evening. The next morning, George having gone ahead, I preached to about five thousand there. It rained violently at five in the evening. Notwithstanding that, two or three thousand people stayed. I expounded to them on that glorious vision of Ezekiel about the resurrection of the dry bones. On Monday, after preaching to two or three thousand, I returned to Bristol and preached to about three thousand.

Crack-Brained for the Gospel's Sake

Tuesday I rode to Bradford, five miles from Bath, where I had long been invited to come. I visited the minister and asked permission to preach in his church. He said it was not usual to preach on the weekdays, but if I could come there on a Sunday, I could assist him. Then I went to a gentleman in the town, who had been present when I preached at Bath. There, with the strongest marks of sincerity and affection, he had wished me good luck in the name of the Lord. Now it was all changed and I found him quite cold. He began disputing on several points. At last he told me plainly that one from my own college had informed him I was always considered a little crack-brained at Oxford.

However, others were not of his mind, so we chose a convenient place, called Bearfield or Buryfield, on the top of the hill overlooking the town below. I offered Christ to about a thousand people—for wisdom, righteousness, sanctification and redemption. Then I returned to Bath and preached on Acts 16:30, "What must I do to be saved?" to a larger audience than ever before.

With so many opportunities to preach to attentive audiences, I wondered why Satan seemed so inactive, when at my return from the place of preaching, the owner told me he could not let me preach anymore on his property. When I asked him why, he said the people hurt his trees and stole things out of his ground. "Besides," he added, "I have already, by letting you be there, earned the displeasure of my neighbors."

I Take Up My Cross

The last Monday in August, I took up my cross by arguing for two hours with a zealous man, laboring to convince him that

142 / *The Nature of Revival*

I was not an enemy of the Church of England. He admitted I taught no other doctrines than those of the church, but could not forgive me for teaching outside church buildings. Indeed, the report now current in Bristol was that I was a Roman Catholic, if not a Jesuit. Some added that I was born and bred at Rome, which many wholly believed.

When visiting my mother, I asked whether her father, Dr. Annesley, had the same faith we preached and if she had heard him preach it to others. She answered he had it for himself. He declared a little before his death that for more than forty years he had no darkness, no fear, no doubt at all of his being accepted in the Beloved. But, nevertheless, she did not remember having heard him preach explicitly on the new birth. She supposed he looked upon it as the peculiar blessing of a few, not being promised to all the people of God.

At Dowgate Hill there were many more than the meeting-houses could contain. Several persons who were convinced of sin came to me the next day. Another, who had been mourning her sin for a long time, earnestly asked us to pray with her. We had scarcely begun to pray when Satan began to tear her so that she screamed out, as if in the pangs of death. Our intercession was short, for within a quarter of an hour she was full of the peace that passes all understanding.

A Living Testimony

On the first Thursday in September, I was sent for by one who had begun to feel she was a sinner. However, a distinguished lady came in unexpectedly, so there was scarcely time for me to speak. When I was free to continue, I noticed a poor, uncultured girl, who was beginning to tell what God had done for her soul. The others looked at one another in amazement, but did not say anything. I then exhorted them not to cease from crying to God till they, too, could say, as she did, "My Beloved is mine, and I am His: I am as sure of it as I am sure that I am alive. For His Spirit bears witness with my spirit that I am a child of God."

Sunday the ninth, I declared to about ten thousand in Moorfields what they must do to be saved. My mother went with us. At about five, my mother accompanying me, we went to Kennington, where there were twenty thousand people waiting for me. I again insisted on that foundation of all our hope: "Believe on the Lord Jesus Christ, and thou shalt be saved" (Acts 16:31).

In the evening I went to our society at Fetter Lane and exhorted them to love one another. The lack of love was a general complaint among them. As we laid it out before the Lord, we soon found He had sent us an answer of peace. Evil surmisings vanished, and the flame kindled again as at the first, knitting together our hearts.

True to the Doctrines

In mid-September a serious clergyman wanted to know on what points we differed from the Church of England. I answered that we had none to the best of my knowledge. The doctrines we preach are the doctrines of the Church of England. The fundamental doctrines of the church are clearly laid down in her prayers, articles, and homilies.

"In what points, then," he asked, "do you differ from the other clergy of the Church of England?"

I answered, "In none from that part of the clergy who adhere to the doctrines of the Church, but from those who dissent though they don't admit it, I differ."

Two weeks later, after I preached once more at Plaistow, I left that place. As I was leaving, a man galloping swiftly rode full into me and overthrew both me and my horse, but without any hurt to either. Glory be to Him who saves both man and beast!

Thursday afternoon, the 27th, I went first to a society at Deptford, and then to Turner's Hall, which holds two thousand persons. The crowd, within and without, was very large. As I began preaching, the main beam which supported the floor broke. The floor immediately sank, causing much noise and confusion among the people. Fortunately, two or three days before, a man had filled the cellar with hogsheads of tobacco. So the floor, after sinking a foot or two, rested upon them and I went on without interruption.

The next day I met with fresh proof that whatsoever you ask believing, you shall receive. A middle-aged woman asked me to return thanks for her to God. Many witnesses testified that she was really distracted a day or two before, and was restrained in her bed. After prayer for her, she was instantly healed and restored to a sound mind.

"What Must I Do to Be Saved?"

At Gloucester I trust a few, out of the two or three thousand, were awakened by the explanation of those words: "Ye have not received the spirit of bondage again to fear; but ye have received the Spirit of adoption, whereby we cry, Abba, Father!" (Rom. 8:15). About eleven I preached at Runwich, about seven miles from Gloucester. The church was very crowded, though a thousand or more stayed in the churchyard. In the afternoon I explained further the same words, "What must I do to be saved?" (Acts 16:30).

Between five and six, I stood on a little green near the town of Stanley and admonished about three thousand to accept Christ. I was strengthened to speak as never before, and continued for nearly two hours. The darkening night and a little lightning didn't lessen the number; it only increased the seriousness of the hearers. I concluded the day by expounding part of our Lord's Sermon on the Mount to a small, serious company at Ebly.

On Monday, October 8, about eight, I reached Hampton Common, nine or ten miles from Gloucester. There I spoke to about five or six thousand persons. I would gladly have stayed longer with these loving people, but I was short of time. After the sermon I hastened away, arriving in Bristol in the evening.

Old Things Pass Away

In Bristol Charles and I were encouraged by the conversion of a notorious drunkard and common swearer. Christ washed him clean, and old things have passed away. In the evening the Lord's power was extended to many who were wounded, bringing healing in His wings. Others, who till then were careless and at ease, felt the two-edged sword that comes out of His mouth.

On Friday, October 12, we had fresh occasion to observe the darkness which has fallen on many who lately rejoiced in God. But God did not long hide His face from them. On Wednesday the spirit of many revived. On Thursday evening many more found Him to be a present help in time of trouble. Never do I remember the power of God being more eminently present than this morning when a cloud of witnesses declared His breaking the gates of brass and smiting the bars of iron in sunder.

I could not help but be concerned with one or two persons who were tormented in an unaccountable manner. They seemed almost lunatic. While I was wondering what could have caused these conditions, I received the answer from the Word of God. "Glory to God in the highest, and on earth peace, goodwill toward men" (Luke 2:14).

At four I preached near the Fishponds at the desire of one who had long labored under the fear that he had blasphemed against the Holy Spirit. I showed him that blasphemy against the Spirit is, according to the plain scriptural account, the open and malicious assertion that the miracles of Christ were wrought by the power of the devil.

Saturday was spent with one who, in deep anguish of spirit, had asked a clergyman's advice the day before. The minister told the woman her head was out of order and she needed to take some medicine. In the evening we called on God for His medicine to heal those who were broken in heart. She, as well as five others who had long been in the shadow of death, knew the war was over and they had passed from death into life. The sharp frost in the morning of Sunday, October 14, did not prevent about fifteen hundred from being at Hannam.

Preaching Plain, Old Religion in Wales

Monday, in response to a pressing invitation I had received some time before, I set out for Wales, and before two arrived at Abergavenny.

Somehow I felt a strong aversion to preaching there. However, I went to the person on whose property George Whitefield preached and asked if I might use it, in case the minister was not willing to let me use the church. On being refused the use of the church, he invited me to his house. About a thousand people stood patiently in the sharp frost after sunset while I simply described the plain, old religion of the Church of England from Acts 28:22, which is now almost everywhere spoken against under the new name of Methodism.

On Wednesday the frost was sharper than before; however, five or six hundred people stayed to hear the sermon. I explained the nature of salvation, which is through faith and faith alone, and the nature of living faith through which this salvation comes. About noon I came to Usk, where I preached to a small company of poor people. One gray-headed man wept and trembled exceedingly. Another who was there, as well as two or three who were at the Devauden, has become quite distracted from the world. They all mourn and refuse to be comforted till they have redemption through His blood.

When I came to Pontypool in the afternoon, I was unable to procure a more convenient place than the street. So I stood and cried aloud to five or six hundred attentive hearers to believe in the Lord Jesus that they might be saved. In the evening I showed His willingness to save all who desire to come unto God through Him. Many were melted into tears.

On Her Way Rejoicing

When we were at the Devauden on Monday, a poor woman who lived six miles off came there in great heaviness. She was deeply convinced and weary of sin, but found no way to escape from it. She walked from Devauden to Abergavenny on Tuesday, and on Wednesday from Abergavenny to Usk. Then in the afternoon, she came to Pontypool. Between twelve and one in the morning, after a sharp contest for her soul, our Lord himself got the victory. The love of God was shed abroad in her heart, and she knew her sins were forgiven and went on her way rejoicing.

Friday I preached in the morning at Newport to the most insensible, ill-behaved people I have ever seen in Wales. One ancient man, during most of the sermon, cursed and swore almost incessantly. Toward the conclusion of my message, he took up a great stone, which he many times attempted to throw but could not. Such are the champions, and such are the arms against field-preaching!

At four I preached at the Shire Hall of Cardiff again, where many gentry were present. I have seldom had such freedom of speech as was given me in explaining those words, "The kingdom of God is not meat and drink; but righteousness, and peace and joy in the Holy Spirit" (Rom. 14:17). At six almost the whole town (I was later informed) came together and I explained the six last Beatitudes. My heart was so enlarged I couldn't stop, so we continued for three hours.

"I Cannot Be Saved!"

On October 23, I was exceedingly drawn to go back to see a young woman in Kingswood. She was nineteen or twenty years old, but could neither read nor write. I found her in bed, being restrained by two or three persons holding her. It was a terrible sight. Anguish, horror, and despair above all description appeared in her pale face. The thousand distortions of her whole body showed how the demons of hell were gnawing her heart. The shrieks intermixed with the speech were hard to endure. But her stony eyes could not weep.

She screamed out as soon as words could find their way, "I am damned, damned, lost forever! Six days ago you might have helped me. But it is past. I am the devil's now. I have given myself to him. I am his. I must serve him. With him I must go to hell. I will be his. I will serve him. I will go with him to hell. I cannot be saved. I will not be saved. I must, I will, I will be damned!" She then began praying to the devil.

We began praying, "Arm of the Lord, awake, awake!"

She immediately sank down as if asleep, but as soon as we stopped, she broke out again with inexpressible vehemence, "Stony hearts, break! I am warning you. Break, break, poor stony hearts! Will you not break? What can be done more for stony hearts? I am damned that you may be saved. Now break, now break, poor stony hearts! You need not be damned, though I must."

She then fixed her eyes on the corner of the ceiling and said, "There he is, yes, there he is! Come, good devil, come! Take me away. You said you would dash my brains out. Come, do it quickly. I am yours. I will be yours. Come just now. Take me away."

We interrupted her by calling again upon God. She sank down as before, and another young woman began to roar out as loud as this one had done. When Charles arrived, it was about nine o'clock. He joined us in prayer and continued till past eleven when God in a moment spoke peace into the soul— to the first one tormented, and then to the other. They both joined in singing praise to Him who had stilled the enemy and the avenger.

The Oppressor Strikes Again

Saturday I was requested to come to Kingswood again to see a woman who had been very ill before. A violent rain began just as I set out, drenching me in a few minutes. While I was still three miles off, the woman cried out, "Yonder comes Wesley, galloping as fast as he can." When I came, I was cold and numb, and more fit for sleep than prayer.

As I entered the house, the woman burst out into horrid laughter and said, "No power, no power, no faith, no faith. She is mine, her soul is mine. I have her and will not let her go."

We begged God to increase our faith. Meanwhile her pangs increased more and more. One would have imagined that her body must have been shattered to pieces by the violence of the throes.

Being clearly convinced this was no natural disorder, I said, "I think Satan is loose. I fear he will not stop here." I added, "I command you, in the name of the Lord Jesus, to tell if you have commission to torment any other soul."

Immediately the answer came, "I have, L.C. and S.J."—two women who lived at some distance and were then in perfect health.

We began to intercede again, and didn't cease till about six o'clock. Then the woman began singing with a clear, composed voice and a cheerful look, "Praise God, from whom all blessings flow."

The last Sunday of October, I preached once more at Bradford, at one in the afternoon. The violent rains did not hinder the ten thousand from coming to earnestly hear me speak on those solemn words, "I take you to record this day, that I am pure from the blood of all men. For I have not shunned to declare unto you all the counsel of God" (Acts 20:26, 27).

The Oppressor's Final Stand

Returning in the evening, I called at a home in Kingswood. Both L.C. and S.J. were there. It was scarcely a quarter of an hour before the first one fell into a strange agony. Soon after, the other followed.

Words cannot describe the violent convulsions over their

entire bodies. Their cries and groans were too horrid to be born.

One of them, in a strange tone of voice, said, "Where is your faith now? Come, go to prayers. I will pray with you, 'Our Father, which art in heaven.' "

We took the advice, from whoever gave it, and poured out our souls before God till L.C.'s agonies so increased that it seemed she would die. But at that moment, God spoke. She knew His voice, and both her body and soul were healed.

We continued in prayer till almost one, when S.J.'s voice was also changed, and she began strongly to call upon God. This she did for most of the night. In the morning we renewed our prayers while she was crying continually, "I burn! I burn! Oh, what shall I do? I have a fire within me. I cannot bear it. Lord Jesus, help!"

Amen, Lord Jesus, Thy time is come.

8

George Whitefield: Speaking As a Prophet*

On Monday, June 4, 1739, I went a second time to pay my respects to the Archbishop of Canterbury, but, as before, he was not home. I visited the Bishop of London, who treated me very well. I took leave of my weeping friends and went with many of them to Blackheath, where there was nearly as large a congregation as at Kennington the last Lord's Day. I don't think I have ever been so anointed since I have begun preaching in the fields. My discourse lasted nearly two hours, and the people were so melted down and wept so loudly that they almost drowned out my voice. I could not help but cry out, *"Come, you Pharisees. Come and see the Lord Jesus himself getting the victory."* Afterward, I went to an inn upon the Heath, where many came in tears to say a last farewell. The remainder of the evening I spent with several of my brethren then went to bed about midnight, thankful for the great things we had seen and heard.

On Sunday, June 10, I hastened to Blendon, from where some of our brethren had come last night to see me. I preached

---

*George Whitefield, *op. cit.,* Fourth Journal, pp. 179–206, June 1739 through August 1739.

with more power than ever, and assisted in administering communion to about two hundred in Bexley Church. I dined, gave thanks, and sang hymns at the Delamottes. Then I preached with great power in the evening on Blackheath to more than twenty thousand people and collected plentifully for the orphans. After the sermon I went to the Green Man Inn, near the place where I preached. I continued till midnight in prayer, praise, thanksgiving and Christian conversation. I believe there were nearly fifty or sixty of us in all. Numbers stood by as spectators. God enlarged my heart greatly in prayer and exhortation. Many of them stayed in prayer and praise all night.

I think it is every Christian's duty to be particularly careful to honor and glorify God where He is dishonored. Some revelers sing the songs of drunkards in public houses. Other sinners spend whole nights in harlotry and wantonness. Why should Christians be ashamed to sing the songs about Jesus and spend nights, as their Lord did, in exercises of devotion?

20,000 Hear Me in the Fields

The following Tuesday evening I preached to about twenty thousand people at Blackheath, and spent the remaining part of the night with more friends.

Wednesday morning, June 13, I went to Blendon, where I preached, and as usual, at Blackheath. Then I went with my fellow travelers to Lewisham, to the house of a woman who had frequently invited me to stay. God raises up unsought-for friends for me in every place! After supper I expounded to and prayed with several whom my hostess had invited to hear the Word. *Oh, that it may take deep root in their hearts!*

On Thursday I spent the whole day in retreat at Blendon. In the evening I had the pleasure of introducing my honored friend, John Wesley, to preach at Blackheath. After the sermon, we spent the evening most agreeably together with many Christian friends at the Green Man Inn. About ten we admitted all who would come in, and the room was soon filled. I exhorted and prayed for nearly an hour and then went to bed, rejoicing that another fresh inroad had been made into Satan's territories by John Wesley's following me in field-preaching in London as well as Bristol.

On Monday, June 18, I learned I would be delayed in embarking to America because of an embargo being laid on shipping. I had time to go to Hertford, where I had been invited by several pressing letters declaring how God had worked by my ministry when I was there last. At eight, I preached, as scheduled, to about four thousand silent and attentive people. I found myself much stronger than when I was here last.

The next day I preached in the morning at about seven to nearly three thousand people. Many came to me under strong conviction of their fallen condition and their lack of Christ as their Mediator. Many had been much moved by my preaching. I preached at 7:00 in the evening to about five thousand souls on the faith of Abraham.

Violently Persecuted

On Wednesday, June 20, I set out about five o'clock in the morning and hastened to Broad Oaks. We got there at about noon and perceived that Providence had sent us to a family, some of whom were born of the Spirit. They are most violently persecuted by those of their own household who are not born again. A clergyman has been employed to divert the saved from their "spiritual madness", as some call it. This minister has done them the honor of preaching against them. For this past week, they have been constantly harassed by many who are lovers of pleasure more than lovers of God. Those opposers tell them that a decent, fashionable religion is sufficient to carry them to heaven. We rejoiced greatly in the prospect of suffering for Christ's sake.

To increase our satisfaction, William Delamotte, a convert of Benjamin Ingham, came from Cambridge to meet us. He is scandalously opposed at that university because of his new faith. The students make him a proverb of reproach, and abuse him in the rudest manner. He has been forbidden entry into one college and two or three who associate with him have been threatened for keeping him company.

The following day I preached twice at Saffron Walden to about two thousand people. I returned to Broad Oaks singing and praising God. Wherever I go, people are drawn to the doctrine of Jesus Christ. "My sheep hear my voice. A stranger will they not follow" (John 10:27, 5).

The last Sunday of June I read prayers and assisted in administering communion at Bexley Church. Many came from afar and expected to hear me speak but the bishop had insisted on the vicar's denying me the pulpit. If we have done anything worthy of the censure of the church, why don't the bishops call us to a public account? If not, why don't they confess and accept us? It is well we can confess to the Great Bishop of our souls.

The bishops say our going out into the highways and bridges and compelling poor sinners to come in is not proper. We ought not to plead so for them to be reconciled to God. They want to know by what authority we preach. They ask, "What sign shewest thou unto us, seeing that thou doest these things?" (John 2:18).

What further sign would they require? We did not go into the fields until we were excluded from the churches. Has not God set His seal to our ministry in an extraordinary manner? Have not many who were spiritually blind received their sight? Have not many who have been lame strengthened to run the way of God's commandments? Have not the deaf heard? the lepers been cleansed? the dead raised? and the poor had the Gospel preached to them? That these notable miracles have been wrought, not in our own names or by our own power, but in the name and by the power of Jesus of Nazareth cannot be denied. And yet they require a sign.

Pulpit to Pasture

In the afternoon I preached to about three hundred people in Justice Delamotte's pasture. In the evening I preached on John 9:34, "And they cast Him out," on Blackheath to about twenty thousand. I recommended to the people the example of the blind beggar and reminded them of preparing for the gathering storm. I exhorted them in the name of Christ Jesus to follow the example of the Lamb of God if my enemies should think that they did God service by killing me. God grant that we may learn when we are reviled not to revile in return. When we suffer, may we not threaten but commit our souls into the hands of Him who judges righteously. *Lord, endue us with the spirit of your first martyr, Stephen, that we may pray most earnestly for our very murderers.*

Later in June I visited the minister of the parish and asked him for the use of his pulpit. He refused it because I did not have my letter of orders. I went to public worship at eleven and afterward preached to about three thousand people in a field near the town. I was later visited by several from the Baptist congregation who brought offerings for the Orphan House.

I set out about four in the afternoon and reached Gloucester about seven in the evening, to the inexpressible joy of many. A recent report of my being dead has only served to make my present visits more welcome. "All things work together for good to them that love God" (Rom. 8:28).

Saturday, June 30, I preached at about ten in the morning to nearly two thousand people in the bowling green belonging to the George Inn at Stroud. God was with us. After the sermon, I went to Gloucester, where I preached at seven in the evening to a larger and more affected congregation than ever.

Sunday was busy. I preached at seven in the morning to a much increased audience in a field. I breakfasted and preached at eleven in the morning, read prayers in the afternoon, and later preached again in Randwick Church. The church was quite full, with about two thousand people outside in the churchyard. By taking down the window behind the pulpit, all were able to hear.

After this service, I hastened to Hampton Common. To my great surprise I found no less than twenty thousand, on horseback and on foot, ready to receive me. I spoke with greater freedom than I had done all the day before. About twelve at night, I reached Gloucester much fresher than I had left it in the morning. Surely Jesus Christ is a gracious Master. They that wait upon Him shall renew their strength.

Nearly Arrested

Monday, after dinner, I went to Tewkesbury. There I found that much opposition had been made to the bailiff against my coming. Upon entering the town, I found the people alarmed. As soon as I was in the inn, four constables came to confront me. A lawyer there, who was my friend, demanded the constable's warrant. Not being able to produce one, they were sent about their business by the lawyer. At eight o'clock I went outside of the town into a field loaned to me for a meeting. My audience consisted of about two or three thousand people. I spoke with freedom and most went away affected. I rejoice that God has led me on from conquered to conquering.

At Tewkesbury on Tuesday, I went to see one of the town bailiffs. I meekly asked him why he had sent the constables to arrest me. He said, "It was the determination, not of myself, but of all the council." He then added, "The people were noisy, and it reflected upon the bailiffs."

I answered, "They were noisy because the constables had been sent to arrest me if I should come into the town."

Upon hearing this, he began to be a little angry and told me, "One judge said he would arrest you as a vagrant if you were to preach near him."

I answered, "He is very welcome to do as he pleases, but no magistrate has power to stop my preaching—even in the streets, if I think it proper."

"No, sir," said he, "and if you preach here tomorrow, we will have the constables arrest you."

After this I took my leave, telling him, "I think it my duty, as a minister, to inform you that magistrates are intended to be a terror to evildoers and not to those who do well." I asked him to be as careful to send constables to the next horse races, balls, and other rowdy assemblies.

On Wednesday, about five in the evening, I saw the town much alarmed. The streets were crowded with people from all parts. I rode straight through the town and preached to about six thousand hearers in a field loaned to us, but saw no constables either to arrest me or molest me.

On Thursday, at Gloucester, at about ten in the morning I preached to a large and greatly affected audience. My own heart was full of love for my dear countrymen. They sincerely sympathized with me. After this, many friends who had to leave to return home told me what God had done for their souls. Having written in my journal and dispatched my private business, I joined in prayer and singing with many before I left Gloucester. About five in the evening I reached Chafford Common and at seven preached till it was nearly dark to about ten thousand people—a glorious increase since I was last there.

"God Is Truly with Us"

Saturday, July 7, I returned to Bristol. I had a useful conference about many things with my honored friend, John Wesley. I found Bristol had great reason to bless God for his ministry. The congregations are much more serious and concerned than when I left them. Their loud and repeated amens put up to every petition, as well as the exemplariness of their common life, plainly show that they have received the grace of God. It is evident that great good is being done here by either an evil or a good spirit. If you say by an evil spirit, it is little less than blasphemy against the Holy Spirit. Slander of the great work that has been wrought in so short a time is from the devil.

On Sunday I preached at the bowling green to about ten thousand people. They were greatly affected indeed. About eleven, I preached again at Hannam Mount to nearly as many and at seven in the evening to about twenty thousand at Rose Green. I find such a visible change for the better in the congregation since I was here last. That convinces me more and more that God is truly with us. As our opposition increases, I know the manifestations of God's presence among us will increase also.

Earlier I received a letter from the Bishop of Gloucester in which he affectionately admonished me to exercise the authority I received in the manner it was given me. His opinion is that I ought to preach the Gospel only in the congregation in which I was lawfully appointed.

After answering his letter, I preached in the afternoon at the brickyard to about eight thousand people. Afterward I preached to several thousand people in the schoolhouse, where the roof had not yet been put up. They seemed much affected by the Word, even attending the churches and societies when John Wesley is absent from them.

Immediately after the sermon was ended, I went with John and several other friends to Bath, and preached there at seven in the evening to about three thousand people. It rained intermittently, but the people were patient and attentive. I never before had such power given me to speak to the polite scoffers. *Oh, that the scales were removed from the eyes of their minds!*

The Honor of Persecution

I heard today that the town clerk of Bristol did John and me the honor of petitioning the grand jury, at their quarter sessions, to prevent our meetings and to have the riot act read. They ignored him. One who was called to serve on the petty jury offered to pay any fine rather than do anything against us, whom he called true servants of Jesus Christ.

The next night, John and I settled some affairs and united

the two leading societies together. How can I be thankful enough to God for sending me here to see that the seed has been sown in good ground, and that under the ministry of John Wesley it has received great increase. May it still grow with all the increase of God.

On Thursday I was busy most of the day preparing a sermon for the crowd, "On the Indwelling of the Spirit," which I would recommend to all. I preached it in the evening to eight or nine thousand people in the bowling green.

The next day, at seven in the morning, I preached my farewell sermon to a weeping and deeply affected audience. My heart was full and I continued nearly two hours in prayer and preaching. Blessed be God for my coming here to behold some fruits of my labors. Many souls have been strengthened and comforted, many convinced of sin, and I myself have become more established and strong in the Lord. As opposition abounds, so do many consolations much more abound. Who is so good a master as Jesus Christ?

Warned Not to Preach

Arriving at Basingstoke, I was served the following letter from the mayor by the hands of the constable:

> Basingstoke, July 19, 1739
>
> Sir,
>
> Being a civil magistrate in this town, I thought it my duty, for the preservation of the peace, to forbid you, or at least dissuade you, from preaching here. If you persist in it, in all probability it may cause disturbance. I think it is your duty, as a clergyman, as well as mine, to prevent this. If any mischief should ensue, whatever pretense you may afterward make in your own behalf, I am satisfied it will fall on your own head, being timely cautioned by me, who am, sir,
>
> Your most humble servant,
> John Abbott
>
> P.S. The Legislature has wisely made laws for the preservation of the peace. Therefore, I hope, no clergyman lives in defiance of them.

To this I immediately sent the following answer:

Honored Sir,

I thank you for your kind letter. I humbly hope a sense of your duty, and not a fear of man, caused you to write it.

If so, allow me as a clergyman to remind you, honored sir, you ought to be not only a terror to evildoers, but a praise to them that do well. I know of no law against such meetings as mine. If any such law exists, I believe you will think it your duty to apprise me of it so I may not offend. If no law can be produced, I think it my duty as a clergyman to inform you that you ought to protect, and not in any way discourage or permit others to disturb, any assembly of people meeting together purely to worship God.

Tomorrow, honored sir, I hear there is to be an assembly of an entirely different nature [a wrestling revel]. Be pleased to be as careful to have the public peace preserved at that. Prevent profane cursing and swearing and persons breaking the sixth commandment by bruising each other's bodies by cudgelling and wrestling. If you do not do this, I shall rise up against you at the Great Day and be a witness against your partiality.

> I am, honored sir,
> your very humble servant,
> George Whitefield

"You Ought to Preach in a Church"

After breakfast on Friday, July 20, I called in person on the mayor to see what law could be produced against my meetings. As soon as I began to talk with him, I perceived he was a little angry.

"Sir," he said, "you sneered at me in the letter you sent last night. Though I am a butcher, sir, I—"

"Honored sir," I protested, "I honor you as a magistrate, and only desired to know what law could be produced against my preaching. In my opinion there can be none, because there was never any such thing as field-preaching before."

"Sir," he said, "you ought to preach in a church."

"And so I would if your minister would permit me to do so."

"Sir," he said, "I believe you have some sinister ends in view. Why do you go about making a disturbance?"

"I make no disturbance," I answered. "I could not come into your town without being insulted. It was your business, sir, to wait, and if there was any riot in my meetings, then, and not till then, to interpose."

He then said, "Sir, you wrote to me about the revel today— I have decided against it."

"But," said I, "you ought, sir, to go and read the riot act and put an entire stop to it." I then pressed him to show me a law against my meetings, urging that if there had been any law, they would have been stopped long ago.

"That is an odd way of preaching," he answered. "But, sir, I must go away to a fair. Before you came, I had written you another letter, which I will send you yet, if you desire."

After this, I thanked him, paid him the respect due to a magistrate, and took my leave.

"Never is He to Be Worshiped in Brothels"

Soon after I had returned to my quarters, he sent me the following letter:

Basingstoke, July 20, 1739

Reverend Sir,

I received your extraordinary letter, expecting nothing less from so uncommon a genius.

I believe your meetings to be unlawful and have no reason to protect you. My understanding of religion always was, and I hope always will be, that God is to be worshiped in places consecrated and set apart for His service. Never is He to be worshiped in brothels and places where all manner of debauchery may have been committed. How far this is consistent with your actions, I leave you to judge.

As for the other assembly you were pleased to mention, it is contrary to my will. I have never given my consent to it, but discouraged it before your reverendship came to this town. If these cudgellers persist in it, I shall set them upon the same level as you, and think you all breakers of the public peace. You very well know there are penal laws against cursing and swearing, and I wish there were the same against deceit and hypocrisy.

Your appearing against me as a swift witness at the day of judgment, I must admit, is a most terrible thing. It may serve as a bugbear for children or people of weak minds, but believe me, reverend sir, those disguises will have but little weight among men of normal understanding.

Yours,
John Abbott

P.S. I told you I had a letter written. I make bold to send it.

To this I sent the following answer:

Basingstoke, July 20, 1739

Honored Sir,

Does Mr. Mayor do well to be angry? Alas! What evil have I done? I honor you as a magistrate, but as a minister, I am obliged to be no respecter of persons. Your believing my meetings to be unlawful does not make them so. There is no need to protect me when I do not act contrary to any law, civil or ecclesiastical. Be pleased to prove that my meetings are schismatical, seditious, or riotous, and then I will submit.

But you say they are upon unconsecrated ground. Honored sir, let me inform you that God is not confined to places, but seeks those to worship Him who worship in spirit and in truth. Where two or three are gathered together in Christ's name, there will Christ be in the midst of them. The Church, by our ministers in their prayer before their sermons, is defined to be not the church walls, but a congregation of Christian people. Such is mine.

As for judging me, to my own Master I stand or fall. At His dreadful tribunal I will meet you, and then you shall see what is in the heart of

Your very humble servant,
George Whitefield

At about eight o'clock I went into a loaned field to preach. Though I was told I would not go out of Basingstoke alive if I preached there, and another said drums would be beat just by me, I had little or no interruption. God gave me power to speak against reveling, and those few scoffers who were there were not able to resist it. As I came from the field, passing through the churchyard, the scoffers, headed by some of the baser sort, signaled at me as before, and called me strange names, which, I trust, I received in the spirit of our dear Master.

Preaching from the Wrestling Ring

A mile or two from town, I passed several going to the wrestling revel. I immediately rode back to town, got upon the stage erected for the wrestlers, and began to show them the error of their ways. Many seemed ready to hear what I had to say, but one, more zealous for Satan than the rest, and fearing conviction every time I attempted to speak, started the wrestlers repeating their noises. I felt willing to be a sacrifice if I might save some of those to whom I was about to speak. While I was on the stage, one struck me with his cudgel.

At last, finding the devil would not permit them to hear my message, I got off. After such thronging and pushing me, I mounted my horse with the inward satisfaction that I had now begun to attack the devil in his strongest holds, bearing my testimony against the detestable diversions of this generation.

On Saturday, July 21, I set out a little after four in the morning and reached London by breakfast time. I preached in the evening to more than ten thousand at Kennington Common.

Ever since I was abused at Basingstoke, I have had sweet communion with God. When men cast us out, then does Jesus Christ take us up. Who would not be a Christian? There is nothing I desire on earth in comparison with that. I received a pressing invitation to come into Lincolnshire, so I preached, Sunday morning at seven, to about twenty thousand at Moorfields. A greater power than ever was among us. Scoffers and curious persons daily drop off. I hope most who come now do not attend out of curiosity. Never were souls more melted down by the power of God's words, and never did people offer their mites more willingly.

I went to St. Paul's and received communion. I preached in the evening at Kennington Common to about thirty thousand hearers and collected for the coal miners. God gave me great power, and I never opened my mouth so freely against the letter-learned clergymen of the Church of England. Every day I see the necessity of speaking out more and more. God knows my heart; I do not speak out of resentment. I heartily wish all the Lord's servants were prophets. I wish the Church of England were the joy of the whole earth. But I cannot, while I see her sinking into religious ignorance and refined Deism, keep silent against those who cause her to err by their sensual, lukewarm lives and unscriptural superficial doctrines.

Persons wonder at me because I talk of persecution now that the world has become Christian. Alas, were Jesus Christ to come down from heaven at this time, He would be treated now as before. Whoever goes forth to preach the Gospel in His Spirit must expect the same treatment His first apostles received. *Lord, prepare us for all events.*

"Bless God for Field-preaching"

This evening I preached at Hackney Marsh to about two thousand people. I prayed and discoursed for more than two hours with greater demonstration of the Spirit than ever. Every day I have more and more reason to rejoice in what God has done for my own and others' souls. Thousands at the Great Day will have reason to bless God for field-preaching.

On Tuesday, July 24, I dispatched my private affairs, and preached in the evening at Kennington Common, to about fifteen thousand.

Wednesday evening, I preached at Edmonton. The congregation was large and attentive, and I rejoiced in having an opportunity to offer salvation freely to the rich. *Oh, that all in high stations were rich toward God!*

On Thursday I preached to more than ten thousand at Hackney Marsh. I had gone there purposely to discourse because there was to be a horse race in the same field. I had the pleasure of bearing my testimony against such unchristian entertainments. Very few left the sermon to see the race, and some of those who did soon returned. By the help of God, I will still go on to attack the devil in his strongest holds. The common people go to these diversions for lack of knowing better. If we can once draw them from these, their minds will be better prepared to receive the Gospel. *Prosper, O Lord, this work.*

On Sunday, July 29, I preached in the morning in Moorfields. The congregation was much larger than we had last Sunday. I also collected more for the school at Kingswood. I preached at Kennington Common in the evening. God sent us a little rain, but that only washed away the curious. Nearly thirty thousand stood their ground, and God, I believe, watered them with the dew of His heavenly blessing. A visible alteration for the better is daily made in the people. It would take too long to recount how many came under strong conviction of their lostness after the preaching. God has begun and will carry on the good work in their souls.

I was busy all Monday morning in directing those who came asking me what they should do to be saved. On Tuesday I preached on Gen. 3:15 at Newington, near Hackney, to about twenty thousand people. On Wednesday evening, I preached at Marylebone Fields to nearly thirty thousand, then later to Fetter Lane Society.

Scoffers Afraid of Being Overpowered by God

August 2, I preached at Newington to more than twenty thousand people. I came home rejoicing to see what a great work God has done in this city. Scoffers seem afraid to show their heads, being frequently overpowered by God's Word. I hope the time spoken of by the prophet is coming, "Behold, ye among the heathen, and regard, and wonder marvelously: for I will work a work in your days which ye will not believe, though it be told you" (Hab. 1:5).

Friday, August 3, was spent in completing my affairs and saying farewells to my dear friends. I preached in the evening to nearly twenty thousand at Kenningon Common. I chose to discourse on Paul's departing speech in Acts 20 to the elders at Ephesus. People were much affected and almost prevented my making any application. I concluded with a suitable hymn, but could scarcely get to the coach because of the people crowding around to take my hand and give me a parting blessing.

En route from London on Saturday, August 4, I preached at Blackheath to about ten thousand before returning to Blendon. On Sunday I preached in the afternoon to about fifteen hundred in Justice Delamotte's yard. In the evening I spoke to about twenty thousand at Blackheath.

Monday, August 6, I went from Blendon and preached in the evening at Chatham, about eighteen miles from there, to nearly twelve thousand people. I have never observed more decency and order in any place at my first preaching.

Tuesday, August 7, I left Chatham early in the morning, dined at Blendon, and preached in the evening at Blackheath. It rained very much the whole day, but there were about two thousand present. I discoursed on the conversion of Zaccheus the publican. I hope there was joy in heaven over some of my hearers repenting. *Lord, in doing your commandments, there is great reward.*

On Wednesday I slept at Lewisham. Going to Deptford, I went on board the ship which we hallowed by the Word of God and prayers. I preached again at Blackheath to nearly twenty thousand people, this time on the Pharisee and the publican. I felt I needed to take notice of a fundamental mistake of the Bishop of London, published this day in a Pastoral Letter. In it he exhorted his clergy to explain the doctrine of justification by faith by making our good works a necessary condition of it.

Paul, in his Epistle to the Galatians, pronounces a dreadful anathema against the holders of such doctrines. "But though we, or an angel from heaven preach any other gospel unto you than that which we have preached unto you, let him be accursed" (Gal. 1:8).

Again on Thursday, I preached at Blackheath to a very large congregation, then went on board the ship in order to be ready to finish my affairs in the morning. Several groups of friends came to see me and some stayed with me all night. In answer to their prayers, I doubt not that we shall be as safe as Noah in the ark. Every place is alike to those who have the presence of God with them.

Friday I finished my ship business and preached in the evening at Blackheath to a greater congregation than ever. The people, expecting it would be the last time, were much affected, but great rejoicing was heard among them when I told them I should continue to preach till Monday.

On Saturday I began in the spirit of meekness to answer the Pastoral Letter by the Bishop of London. I preached in the evening at Blackheath.

"Farewell!"

My last Sunday I preached early in the morning to some hundreds in Justice Delamotte's pasture, most of whom had come there the night before singing and praising God. I read prayers, heard a truly Christian sermon from Mr. Piers, and assisted him in administering communion to nearly six hundred in his own church. I preached again at three in the afternoon to nearly three thousand at Delamotte's and to about thirty thousand at Blackheath. At each place the people were exceedingly affected. Much devotion and reverence was to be seen during the time of administration of communion. In the afternoon at Blackheath, when I said, "Finally, brethren, farewell!" thousands immediately burst out into strong crying and tears. I continued my discourse till it was nearly dark. With great difficulty I got away in a coach to Lewisham. I retired to rest with a deeper sense of my own sinfulness than I have felt for some time.

On Monday I rose early and hastened to Blendon. I finished my answer to the Bishop's Pastoral Letter and sent it to the press. I dined and took leave of my dear weeping friend. I went from there in a boat to Gravesend to board our ship.

Blessed be God for detaining me in England by the embargo. I trust many others as well as myself have reason to rejoice. *Lord, teach me in all things simply to comply with your will, without presuming to say, even in my heart, "Why do you?"*

9

*Charles Wesley: Doing the Master's Work**

The societies were growing rapidly, and the spirit of delusion quickly followed the converts into our company.

Early in June, I was with George Whitefield at Blendon. Bowers and Bray followed us there, drunk with the spirit of delusion. George honestly said, "They are two grand enthusiasts."

At the society, on Wednesday evening, June 6, Shaw pleaded for his spirit of prophecy and charged me with love of preeminence and with making my proselytes twofold more children of the devil than before. Wolf said he looked upon me as delivered over to Satan. They declared themselves no longer members of the Church of England. By grace we were kept tolerably meek, and parted at eleven. Now I am clear of them. By renouncing the church, they have discharged me.

Pretenders of Inspiration

Many of our friends have been pestered by the French Prophets and similar pretenders to inspiration. John Bray is

---

*Thomas Jackson, *op. cit.,* Vol. 1, pp. 120–139, June 1, 1739 through August 27, 1739.

the foremost to listen to them, and is often carried away with their delusions. Today I had the happiness to find at his house the famous Prophetess Lavington. She was sitting by Bowers with Mrs. Sellers on the other side.

The Prophet Wise asked, "Can a man attain perfection here?"

I answered, "No." The Prophetess began groaning. I turned and said, "If you have anything to speak, speak it."

She lifted her voice, like a Grecian oracle, and cried out vehemently, "Look for perfection. I say absolute perfection!"

I was thinking of rebuking her, but God gave me uncommon recollection and command of spirit, so that I sat quietly and did not reply. I offered at last to sing, which she allowed but did not join. Bray pressed me to stay and hear her pray. They knelt, but I stood. She prayed most pompously, addressing Bray with particular high praise. She concluded with a most horrible, hellish laugh, and endeavored to turn it off. She showed violent displeasure against our baptized Quaker, saying God had shown her He would destroy all outward things.

On Friday and Saturday I took the statements of Anne Graham, Mrs. Biddle, and Mrs. Rigby, concerning Miss Lavington's lewd life and conversation. We warned our friends everywhere against her. Later I joined at West's with Hutchins and Miss Kinchin, in earnest prayer for the promise of the Father.

The Blessing of Opposition

Whitsunday, June 10, I read my account of the Prophetess to the society. All were shocked, except poor John Bray. He now appeared and strongly withstood me to vindicate that Jezebel. I gave no ground to him—not for a moment. My natural temper was kept down and changed into a passionate concern for him, which I expressed in prayers and tears. All except him were melted down. I kissed him, and testified of my love, but could make no impression.

On Monday I expounded with great liberty of spirit and

received the blessing of opposition.

Tuesday, June 12, brought more news of the Prophetess. She told a brother that she can command Christ to come to her in what shape she pleases, such as a dove or an eagle. The devil owed her another shaming by bringing her again to Bray's. Wise, her gallant knight, came first. With a plain question, I asked whether he had cohabited with her. He was forced to confess he had. John Bray was vehement in her defense. When she came in, she flew upon us like a tigress and tried to overcome me. She insisted she was immediately inspired. I prayed.

She cried that the devil was in me, that I was a fool, a blockhead, a blind leader of the blind set to put out the people's eyes. Then she roared outrageously and said it was the lion in her. True, but not the Lion of Judah. She insisted she would come to the society in spite of me. If she did not, they would all go down.

I asked, "Who is on God's side? Who is for the old prophets instead of the new? Let them follow me." They followed me into the preaching room. I prayed, and expounded the lesson with extraordinary power. Several of the women gave an account of their conversion through my ministry. Our dear brother Bowers confessed himself convinced of his error. We rejoiced and triumphed in the name of the Lord our God.

On Wednesday, my brother John returned. We discussed the affair of the Prophetess before the society. Bray and Bowers were much humbled, and all agreed to disown the Prophetess. Brother Hall proposed expelling Shaw and Wolf. We consented that their names should be erased from the society book, because they disowned themselves members of the Church of England.

The next day I heard John preach at Blackheath on "Christ our wisdom, righteousness, sanctification and redemption." We continued at the Green Man Inn, singing and rejoicing. George Whitefield gave a lively exhortation to about thirty of us.

Barred from the Pulpit

The last time I had met Mr. Stonehouse and our opposers in the vestry, he astonished me by telling me he had consented that I should preach no more. I thought to myself, "What is this man? Or what is friendship?" and said nothing.

Today, with my brother and him, I mentioned, without intending it, my exclusion through his consent. He pleaded that the Bishop of London had justified his church wardens in their forcible expulsion of me, but at last was quite melted down and would do anything to repair his mistake. He resolved that no other should be excluded by him, as I had been.

On Sunday, June 17, John preached to more than ten thousand people, as was later estimated, in Moorfields, and to a still larger congregation on Kennington Common. I preached twice in the prison. Monday I sang and prayed at Mrs. Euster's, a lively, gracious soul, but too apt to depend on her inward feelings.

By Tuesday I was at Lambeth with Mr. Piers, when his bishop expressly forbade him to let any of us preach in his church, charging us with breach of the canon. I mentioned the Bishop of London's authorizing my forcible exclusion. He would not hear me and said he did not dispute. He asked me what call I had.

I answered, "A dispensation of the Gospel is committed to me."

"That is, to St. Paul, but I do not dispute. I will not proceed to excommunication, yet," said the bishop.

"Your Grace has taught me in your book on church government that a man unjustly excommunicated is not thereby cut off from communion with Christ."

"Of that, I am the judge," he replied.

I asked him if George Whitefield's success was not a spiritual sign and sufficient proof of his call, and recommended Gamaliel's advice.

He dismissed us both—Piers, with kind professions, and me, with all the marks of displeasure.

Fear of Man Invades My Soul

I felt nothing in my heart but peace, and prayed and sang at Bray's. However, some hours after, at West's, I sank down in great heaviness and discouragement. I found a little relief from the scripture I turned to, Acts 17:3, "Opening and alleging, that Christ must needs have suffered, and risen again from the dead; and that this Jesus, whom I preach unto you, is Christ."

On Friday, June 22, Satan, the sower of tares, began to trouble us with disputes about predestination. John was wonderfully accepted at Wapping, last week, while asserting the contrary truth. Tonight I asked in prayer that if God would have all men to be saved, He would show some token for good to us. Three were born again in immediate answer to that prayer. We prayed again, and several fell down under the power of God, to witness His universal love.

On Saturday some of the persons saved and set at liberty called on me to return thanks to God in their behalf. Twelve received forgiveness last night, and another today in this prayer. My inward conflict continued. I perceived it was the fear of man, and that by preaching in the field next Sunday, as George Whitefield urges me, I shall break down the bridge and become desperate. I retired and prayed for particular direction, offering up my friends, my liberty, and my life for Christ's sake and the Gospel's. I was somewhat less burdened, yet could not be at ease till I gave up all.

Forsaking the Pulpit for the Field

On Sunday, June 23, the first scripture I cast my eye upon was "Then came the servant unto him, and said, Master, what shall we do?" I prayed with West, and went forth in the name of Jesus Christ. I found nearly ten thousand helpless sinners waiting for the Word in Moorfields. I invited them in my Master's words, as well as His name, "Come unto me, all ye that labour and are heavy laden, and I will give you rest" (Mt. 11:28).

The Lord was with me, even me, His lowest messenger, according to His promise. At St. Paul's, the Psalms and lessons for the day put fresh life into me. So did communion. My load was gone, along with all my doubts and scruples. God shone upon my path and I knew this was His will concerning me.

At Newington, the rector, Mr. Motte, asked me to preach. My text was, "All have sinned, and come short of the glory of God: being justified freely by his grace through the redemption that is in Christ Jesus" (Rom. 3:23–24). I walked onto the common and cried to the multitudes, "Repent ye, and believe the Gospel." The Lord was my strength, and my mouth, and my wisdom. "Oh, that men would praise the Lord for his goodness!" (Ps. 107:15).

By Friday I reached Wycombe and heard of much disturbance and sin, occasioned by Bower's preaching in the streets. I went on to Oxford the next day. There I visited the dean, who spoke with unusual severity against George Whitefield and field-preaching. He explained away all inward religion and also union with God.

I have too much proof that the world and their god abhor our behavior. This whole week, the messenger of Satan has been buffeting me with uninterrupted temptation.

Sunday I preached a sermon on justification before the university, with great boldness. All were very attentive. One could not help weeping. That night I received power to expound. Several professors were present, and some of them mocked me.

Oxford Stands Against Methodism

Monday, July 2, John Gambold arrived. He had been with the Vice Chancellor, and was well received by him. I visited the Vice Chancellor, at his own request, and gave him a full account of the Methodists. He approved, but objected to our doing good in other men's parishes. He charged George Whitefield with insincerity and breach of promise. I appealed to the dean and scheduled a second meeting with him. All were against my sermon, saying it was liable to be misunderstood.

Poor wild Bowers had been detained for preaching in Oxford. The sexton brought him to me for correction on Tuesday, and I spoke to him very directly. He had nothing to reply, but promised to preach there no more. By this agreement, he obtained his liberty.

Tuesday night I had another conference with the dean, who condemned George Whitefield to judgment. "Mr. Dean," I said, "he shall be ready to answer your citation."

He used his harshest criticism to try to stop me from preaching abroad, from expounding in houses, and from singing psalms. He denied justification by faith alone and all the vital religion we experienced. He promised me, however, to read both William Law's and Blaise Pascal's works.

I returned to London, and on Sunday morning, July 8, I counted nearly ten thousand who heeded diligently the word I preached in Moorfields, "Thou shalt call his name Jesus: for he shall save his people from their sins." Many seemed greatly affected. Later, while walking over an open field to Kennington Common, I was met by a man named Goter, who threatened me for trespassing.

In the evening I preached "Christ, our wisdom, righteousness, sanctification and redemption" to double my morning congregation. The Lord Almighty bowed their hearts before Him. Many were pierced through with the sword of the Spirit, the Word of God.

Continual Storm of Temptation

I never knew till now the strength of temptation and the energy of sin. Who that conferred with flesh and blood would covet great success? I live in a continual storm. My soul is always in my hand. The enemy thrusts hard at me that I may fall, and the enemy worse than the devil is my own heart. I humbly hope I received a fresh pardon in communion at St. Paul's. I would have preached at the Fleet, but the warden forbade me. Instead, I preached at the Marshalsea jail. Monday I went to Newgate and talked with five condemned malefactors.

The following Wednesday, I was served with a writ by Mr. Goter for walking over his field to Kennington. I sent Oakley to Goter's lawyer, who confessed he did not know why his client was suing me. Later, the Lord applied His Word at Bray's, so that at least one received forgiveness under it.

On Saturday I dined with my friend George Whitefield in Lewisham, and Sunday I again preached in the fields. There, I discoursed on the promise, "I will pray the Father, and he shall give you another Comforter" (John 14:16). My subject was the same at Kennington. In that congregation, we witnessed one woman receiving her pardon. We gave thanks with her, whom the Lord has redeemed.

The next Tuesday was fully occupied. I preached repentance and faith at Plaistow, and at night I expounded in a private house on the death and raising of Lazarus. Wednesday, I called on Thomas Keen with Hodges, a mild and candid Quaker, then went on to preach at Marybone. Being well pleased with my success brought upon me the buffetings of Satan. Finally, I preached on Kennington Common, "Repent ye, and believe the gospel."

Tempted to Stop Preaching

I wrote George Whitefield an account of both my labors and my conflicts:

Dear George,

I forgot to mention the most important occurrence at Plaistow, namely that a clergyman was there convinced of sin. He stood before me and appeared, throughout my discourse, under the strongest uneasiness of mind. On our return, we were much delighted with an old spiritual Quaker, who is clear in justification by faith alone. At Marybone a footman was convinced of more than sin, and now waits with confidence for all the power of faith. My friend Thomas Keen seems to have a vital

Christian experience and is right in the foundation. I cannot preach out of town on the weekdays because of the expense of travel, nor can I accept William Seward's offer. I would be less hesitant if he would take my advice. But while he is so lavish with the Lord's goods, I cannot agree that his expenses should in any degree seem to be caused by me. I am continually tempted to stop preaching and hide myself like John Hutchins. I would then be freer from temptation and at leisure to attend my own improvement. God continues to work through me, but not in me in any way I can perceive. Please do not reason with me, my brother, in the work God is doing. I cannot expect He should long employ one who is ever longing and murmuring to be discharged. But I do rejoice in your success, and pray for its increase a thousand-fold.

"Ignore Your Comforts"

Today I took John Bray to meet William Law. Law resolved all his feelings and experiences into fits, or natural reactions, and advised Bray to ignore his comforts, which he was better without. Law blamed George Whitefield's journals and his way of preaching. He said he'd had great hopes that the Methodists would have been dispersed little by little into pastorates, and have leavened the whole lump. I then told him my experience.

"If you are right, then I am far below you," said Law, "and not worthy to bear your shoes."

He agreed to our notion of faith, but believes all men hold it. He was fully against laymen expounding as the very worst thing, both for themselves and others.

I told him he was my schoolmaster, used to bring me to Christ, but the reason I did not come to Him sooner was my seeking to be made perfect before I was born again. I disclaimed all expectation of becoming someone great.

Among other things he said, "Was I so talked about as George Whitefield, I would run away and hide myself entirely."

"You might," I answered, "but God would bring you back like Jonah."

"Joy in the Holy Spirit," he told us, "is the most dangerous thing God could give."

I replied, "But cannot God guard His own gifts?"

He often disagreed and commented, "Seeing you have the Spirit of God . . ." He finally began to change a bit, and at last came almost quite over.

"I Was So Buffeted . . ."

On Sunday, I received great power to explain the parable of the Good Samaritan. I received communion at St. Paul's, as I do every Sunday. I convinced multitudes at the common from: "Such were some of you: but ye are washed" (1 Cor. 6:11). Before the day was past, I felt my own sinfulness so great that I wished I had never been born.

Monday, August 13, I wrote, in a letter to William Seward, of this:

> I preached yesterday to more than ten thousand hearers. I was so buffeted by feelings of inadequacy, both before and after, that, was I not forcibly detained, I would have fled from every human face. If God does make a way for me to escape, I shall not easily be brought back again. I do not like the advertising. It seems like sounding a trumpet.

On Tuesday, August 14, I took Cossart, a Moravian, to meet William Law and left them together. Later, the whole congregation at Kennington seemed so moved by my discourse on the words, "He will reprove the world of sin, and of righteousness, and of judgment" (John 16:8), that I could hardly get away from them. We hear every day of more and more convinced or pardoned.

"Let Not His Opinion Weaken Your Hands"

The next day I wrote to George Whitefield:

> Let not Cossart's negative opinion of your letter to the bishop weaken your hands. It is the Moravian infirmity. Tomorrow I set out for Bristol. I pray you all a good voyage, and that many poor souls may be added to the church by your ministry before we meet again. I am confident we shall meet again,

perhaps both here and in America. The will of the Lord be done with us and by us, in time and in eternity.

Later, I called on our brother Bell, just as his wife received the precious faith. We all celebrated her joy.

Thursday I rode to Wycombe. Being refused the church, I would have preached in a house, but Bowers' preaching here has shut the door against me by confirming their natural aversion to the Gospel. The next day we came to Oxford, and the day after that to Eversham. I sent accounts of our going on from time to time to my brother and friends. The following letter was sent to my brother John.

In George Whitefield's Pulpit

Dear Brother,

We left the brethren at Oxford much edified, and two students, besides Charles Graves, were thoroughly awakened. On Saturday afternoon God brought us to Eversham. William Seward was away from home, so there was no admittance for us. His wife is an opposer, and refused to see George Whitefield and me. At seven, William found us at our inn, and took us to his home. I expounded at eight in the schoolroom, which held two hundred, and there held out the promise of the Comforter from John 16.

On Sunday morning I preached from George Whitefield's pulpit, the roadside wall, "Repent ye, and believe the Gospel." The notice being short, we had only a few hundred, but just as those described in the morning lesson, these were more noble than those of Thessalonica, in that they received the word with all readiness of mind. In the evening I offered the Savior to nearly two thousand after expanding on the Good Samaritan.

Many, I am persuaded, found themselves stripped, wounded, and half dead, and are therefore ready for the oil and wine. Once more, God strengthened me at nine to open the New Covenant at the schoolhouse, which was crowded with deeply attentive sinners.

"Beat Me As Long As You Please"

On Monday I spoke from Acts 2:37 to two or three hundred marketpeople and soldiers, all as orderly and decent as could be desired. I now heard that the mayor had come down on Sunday to investigate us. Soon after, an officer struck a country man in the face without any provocation. A serious woman besought the poor man not to resist evil, as the other only wanted to cause a riot. He patiently took several repeated blows, telling the officer he might beat him as long as he pleased.

I took a walk with William Seward, whose eyes God has been pleased to open and see that He would have all men to be saved. His wife, who refuses to see me, is miserably bigoted to the predestination teaching.

We had the satisfaction of meeting with William's cousin Molly, whom I endeavored to convince of sin at Islington. The Spirit has now convinced her of righteousness in Christ. Today she told us a young lady, here upon a visit, had been deeply struck by the Word on Sunday night, seeing and feeling her need of our Physician, and earnestly desiring me to pray for her. We immediately joined in Thanksgiving and intercession. After dinner I spoke with her. She burst into tears and told us she had come here thoughtless, dead in pleasures and sin, and fully resolved against ever being a Methodist. At first she was alarmed at seeing us so happy and full of love, but had gone to the society. She never found out about herself till the Word came with power to her soul. All the following night she had been in agony. She could not pray, nor bear our singing, nor have any rest in her spirit. We took ourselves to prayer and God listened. She received forgiveness in that instant and triumphed in the name of the Lord her God. All of us were greatly filled with joy the rest of the day.

At six I explained the nature of faith from Gal. 2:20: "Not I, but Christ liveth in me . . . Who loved me, and gave himself for me." Afterward, in the schoolhouse, I showed them their own case in dead Lazarus. Some of those that were dead, I trust, began to come forth. Several serious people from the neighboring towns came home with us, where we continued our rejoicing till midnight.

The Genuine Mark of His Disciples

The following Tuesday, I begged my hearers to be reconciled unto God. I found the lady who had been greatly strengthened by last night's expounding. I could hardly keep from crying out that she had been that Lazarus, and if they would come to Christ, He would raise them as He had her. All night she continued singing in her heart, and discovered more and more of that genuine mark of His disciples: love.

I was prevailed upon to stay over for the day. God soon showed us His design in it. Our singing in the garden drew two sincere women to us who sought Christ in sorrow. After reading the promises in Isaiah, we prayed and they received Christ and the promises for themselves. Through the joy with which our Master filled us, we were on a spiritual mountain which reminded us of Tabor. How shall I be thankful enough for His bringing me here?

While we were singing, a poor drunken servant of William Seward's was struck. Last night William had given him warning, and now he seems effectually called. We spent the afternoon most delightfully in Isaiah. At seven the society met. I could hardly speak because of my cold, but it was suspended while I showed the natural man his picture in blind Bartimeus. Many were ready to cry after Jesus for mercy. The three who had lately received their spiritual sight were much strengthened. One declared her salvation before two hundred witnesses, many of whom were pleasure-loving young gentlewomen. They received her testimony, flocked round about her, and pressed her on all sides with requests to come to see them. By this open confession, she purchased for herself great boldness in the faith.

On Wednesday morning, the work of poor Robin, the servant, appeared to be God's work. The words that first made impression on me were: " 'Tis mercy all, immense and free; for, O my God, it found out me!"

He now seems full of sorrow, joy, astonishment, and love. The world, too, confirmed that he belongs to Christ.

Predestined by Apathy

Here I cannot but observe the narrow spirit of those who hold only predestined redemption. I have no disputes with them, yet they see me as an abomination. Mrs. Seward is irreconcilably angry with me because I offer Christ to all. Her maids are of the same spirit and their Baptist teacher insists that I ought to have my gown stripped over my ears.

When William, in my hearing, exhorted one of the maids to a concern for her salvation, she answered, "It is to no purpose. I can do nothing." He received the same answer from his seven-year-old daughter.

On August twenty-fifth, before I went out into the streets and highways, I sent a request to use the church as usual. The minister, one of the better disposed, sent back a courteous message that he would be glad to drink a glass of wine with me, but would not lend me his pulpit for any price.

My Strength Renewed

George Whitefield loaned me his field, which did just as well. For nearly an hour and a half, God gave me voice and strength to exhort about two thousand sinners to repent and believe the Gospel. My voice and strength failed together. I do not want or need them when my work is done. Being invited to Painswick, I waited upon the Lord and renewed my strength. We found nearly one thousand gathered in the street.

I have but one subject. I discoursed from 2 Cor. 5:19: "God was in Christ, reconciling the world unto himself." I besought them earnestly to be reconciled, and the rebels seemed inclined to lay down their arms. A young Presbyterian teacher also came over to us. Then I received fresh strength to expound on the Good Samaritan at a public house, which was full upstairs and down.

On Saturday, in the street, I showed the promise made to them and to their children. Some are, I trust, on the point of receiving it. Three clergymen came to listen. I prayed with a young woman who was afraid of death because to her it had not lost its sting. I showed her the promise was to those that are afar off, even before they actually receive it, if they can but trust that they shall receive it. This revived her greatly and we left her patiently waiting for the salvation of God.

At nine I exhorted and prayed with a house full of sincere souls, and upon leaving, I was recommended by their affectionate prayers to the grace of God.

Preaching to My Mob

At Gloucester, I went to the field at five. An old intimate acquaintance stood in my way and challenged me, "What, Mr. Wesley! Is it you I see? Is it possible that you who can preach at Christ Church, St. Mary's, and elsewhere, would then come here before a mob?"

I cut her short, "The work which my Master gives me must I not do it?" and went to my mob, or to put it in the Pharisees' phrase, "this people who . . . are cursed" (John 7:49).

Thousands heard me gladly while I told them of their privilege of the Holy Spirit, the Comforter, and exhorted them to come to Christ as poor, lost sinners. I continued my discourse till nightfall.

Sunday the minister here at Runwick lent me his pulpit. I stood at the window, which was taken down, and turned to the larger congregation of more than two thousand in the churchyard. They appeared greedy to hear, while I testified, "God so loved the world, that he gave his only begotten Son" (John 3:16).

After the sermon, a woman who had received faith by hearing George Whitefield, came to me. She was terrified at having lost her comfort. I explained to her about the wilderness into which the believer is generally led by the Spirit to be tempted as soon as he is baptized with the Holy Spirit. This confirmed in her a patient anticipation of the return of Him whom her soul loves.

In the afternoon, I preached again to a Kennington congregation. The church was filled to capacity, with thousands standing in the churchyard. It was the most beautiful sight I had ever beheld. The people filled the gradually rising area which was shut up on three sides by a vast perpendicular hill. On the top and bottom of the hill was a circular row of trees. They stood in this amphitheater, deeply attentive, while I called upon them in Christ's words, "Come unto me, all ye that labour and are heavy laden" (Matt. 11:28). The tears of many testified that they were ready to enter into that rest. God enabled me to lift up my voice like a trumpet so that all distinctly heard me. I concluded by singing an invitation to sinners.

It was with difficulty that we made our way through this most loving people and returned amid their prayers and blessings to Ebly. Here I expounded the second lesson for two hours, and received strength and faith to plead the promise of the Father. A good old Baptist pressed me to preach at Stanley on my way to Bristol.

The Prince of the Moisture of the Air

Accordingly, on Monday, I set out at seven. The sky was overcast, and the Prince of the moisture of the air wet us to the skin. This, I thought, portended good. We could not wait to dry ourselves because, contrary to our expectations, a company of nearly one thousand waited. I preached from a table, having first been denied the pulpit, on "Repent, and believe the Gospel." The hearers seemed so much affected that I appointed them to meet me again in the evening. I noticed the minister was in the audience.

I rode back to Ebly and was informed Christ had fastened upon a poor prodigal and spoken to his heart. His convictions were heightened by the sermon. We prayed and sang alternately till faith came. God blew with His Spirit, and the living waters flowed. He struck the hard rock, and the waters gushed out, and the poor sinner, with joy and astonishment, believed the Son of God loved him and gave himself for him. "Sing, O ye heavens; for the Lord hath done it: shout, ye lower parts of the earth!" (Isa. 44:23).

Part 4

The Saving Message of Revival

10

*John Wesley: Faith Is the Only Thing**

"To him that worketh not, but believeth on him that justifieth the ungodly, his faith is counted for righteousness" (Rom. 4:5).

How a sinner may be justified before God, the Lord and Judge of all, is a question of great importance to everyone. It is the foundation of all our hope, because while we are apart from God there can be no true peace, no solid joy, either now or in eternity. What peace can there be while our own heart condemns us? Knowing that He is greater than our hearts and knows all things, what joy is there either in this world or that to come while God's judgment is on us?

And yet how little has this important question been understood. Many have had confused ideas concerning it. Indeed, not only confused, but often utterly false ideas, as contrary to the truth as light is to darkness, notions which are absolutely inconsistent with the Word of God and with the whole tradition of faith. Hence, erring about the very foundation, they could not possibly build on it a faith that would endure when tried

---

*John Wesley, A.M., *Sermons on Several Occasions,* (New York: Carlton and Porter, 1857) "Justification by Faith," Sermon V, Vol. 1, p. 34 ff.

as by fire. Theirs is a faith of only hay and stubble, neither acceptable to God nor useful to man.

In order to do justice, as far as I can, to the importance of the subject, I hope to save those who sincerely seek the truth apart from vain suppositions. I shall endeavor to give them true and just conceptions of this great mystery of godliness.

Man Was Made in the Image of God

First, what is the general ground of this whole doctrine of justification? Man was made in the image of God: holy, as He who created him is holy; merciful, as the Author of all is merciful; perfect, as the Father in heaven is perfect. As God is love, so man, dwelling in love, dwelt in God and God in him. God made man to be an image of His own eternity, an incorruptible picture of the God of glory, accordingly pure, as God is pure from every spot of sin. He knew no evil of any kind or degree, and was inwardly and outwardly sinless and undefiled. He loved the Lord his God with all his heart, and with all his mind, soul, and strength. To this upright and perfect man, God gave a perfect law to which He required full and perfect obedience. He required full obedience in every point, performed without any intermission, from the moment man became a living soul till the time his life ended. No allowance was made for any falling short. Indeed, there was no need of any! Man was altogether equal to the task assigned, and thoroughly endowed for every good word and work.

To the entire law of love which was written in his heart, it seemed good to the sovereign wisdom of God to add another, a positive law "But of the tree of the knowledge of good and evil, thou shalt not eat of it," adding that penalty, "for in the day that thou eatest thereof thou shalt surely die" (Gen. 2:17).

Such then was the state of man in Paradise. By the free, unmerited love of God, he was holy and happy. He knew, loved, and enjoyed God, having in substance, life everlasting. In this life of love he was to continue forever if he continued to obey

God in all things. If he disobeyed Him in any, he was to forfeit all. "In that day," said God, "thou shalt surely die" (Gen. 2:17). Man did disobey God. He ate of the tree of which God had commanded him, saying, "Thou shalt not eat of it" (Gen. 2:17). At that moment, he was condemned by the righteous judgment of God. Then the sentence, of which he was warned before, was executed. At the moment he tasted that fruit, he died. His soul was separated from God. Separate from God, the soul has no more life than the body has when separate from the soul. Man's body, likewise, became corruptible and mortal, so that death took hold of this also. Being already dead in spirit, dead to God, and dead in sin, he hastened on to death everlasting, to the destruction both of body and soul in the fire never to be quenched.

"Wherefore, as by one man sin entered into the world, and death by sin; and so death passed upon all men" (Rom. 5:12) as our inheritance from him who was the common father and representative of us all. So, through the offense of one, all are dead—dead to God, dead in sin, dwelling in a corruptible, mortal body, shortly to be dissolved, and under the sentence of death eternal. For as by one man's disobedience, all were made sinners. By the offense of one, judgment came upon all men to condemnation.

The Only Begotten Son Became Man

This was the state of all mankind when God so loved the world that He gave His only begotten Son, so we might not perish, but have everlasting life. In God's time, He was made man, another common Head of mankind and a second general parent and representative of the whole human race. As such, He bore our griefs with the Lord laying upon Him the sins of us all. Then He was wounded for our transgressions, bruised for our iniquities. He made His soul an offering for sin. Jesus Christ poured out His blood for the transgressors, and bore our sins in His own body on the cross so that by His stripes we

192 / *The Nature of Revival*

might be healed. By that one oblation of himself, once offered, He has redeemed me and all mankind, having made a full, perfect, and sufficient sacrifice and satisfaction for the sins of the whole world.

In consideration of this, that Jesus has tasted death for every man, God has now reconciled the world to himself, not charging mankind with trespasses. Thus as by the offense of one, judgment came upon all men to condemnation, so by the righteousness of one the free gift of justification came upon all men. So, for the sake of His Son, because of what Jesus has done and suffered for us, God now promises to both remit the punishment due for our sins, restoring us in His favor, and to restore our dead soul to spiritual life, as the guarantee of eternal life.

This is the general ground of the whole doctrine of justification. By the sin of the first Adam, who was the father and the representative of us all, we all fell short of the favor of God. We all became children of wrath, or as the Bible expresses it, "judgment came upon all men to condemnation" (Rom. 5:18). Then, by the sacrifice for sin made by the second Adam, as the representative of us all, God is reconciled to all the world. He has given us a new covenant. The condition being once fulfilled, now there is no more condemnation for us. We are "justified freely by his grace through the redemption that is in Jesus Christ" (Rom. 3:24).

The Nature of Justification

But what is it to be justified? What is justification? This is the second thing which I propose to show. It is evident, from what has already been observed, that justification is not being made actually just and righteous. That is sanctification, which is, indeed, in some degree, the immediate fruit of justification. Nevertheless, sanctification is a distinct gift of God, of a totally different nature. Justification implies *what God does for us through His Son*. Sanctification is *what He works in us by His*

Spirit. Some rare instances may be found wherein the term *justified* or *justification* is used in so wide a sense as to include sanctification also. Yet, in general use, they are sufficiently distinguished from each other by Paul and other biblical writers.

It is not farfetched conceit to believe that justification clears us from accusation, particularly that of Satan. This is easily provable from any clear text of holy writ. In the whole scriptural account of this matter, neither Satan the accuser nor his accusation appears to be at all included. It cannot be denied that Satan is the accuser of men, and is emphatically so called. But it does in no way appear that the apostle Paul makes any reference to this in all that he has written concerning justification, either to the Romans or the Galatians.

It is also far easier to take for granted than to prove from any clear scripture that justification is clearing us from the accusation brought against us by the law. This unnatural way of speaking about it means nothing less than this: whereas we have transgressed the law of God, and thereby deserve damnation of hell, God does not inflict on those who are justified the punishment which they had deserved.

Least of all does justification imply that God is deceived in those whom He justifies, that He thinks them to be what, in fact, they are not. He never accounts them to be otherwise than they are. It does not imply that God judges concerning us contrary to the real nature of things. He never esteems us better than we really are, or believes us righteous when we are unrighteous. The judgment of the all-wise God is always according to truth. It is inconsistent with His unerring wisdom for Him to think that I am innocent, to judge that I am righteous or holy because another is so. He can no more, in this manner, confuse me with Christ than with David or Abraham. Let anyone to whom God has given understanding consider this without prejudice. One cannot but perceive such a notion of justification is neither reconcilable to reason nor Scripture.

Justification Is Pardon

The plain, scriptural notion of justification is pardon: the forgiveness of sins. It is that act of God the Father in which, for the sake of the propitiation made by the blood of His Son, He shows forth His righteousness and mercy by the remission of past sins. This is the easy, natural account of it given by Paul throughout Romans. He explains it more particularly in chapter five. Thus, in the verses after the text, Paul says, "Blessed are they whose iniquities are forgiven, and whose sins are covered. Blessed is the man to whom the Lord will not impute sin" (Rom. 4:7, 8). To each who is justified or forgiven, God will not impute sin or condemn him. He will not condemn him on that account, either in this world or in that which is to come. His sins—all his past sins, in thought, word, and deed—are covered, are blotted out, shall not be mentioned against him, any more than if they had not been. God will not inflict on that sinner what he deserved to suffer, because Jesus has suffered for him. From the time we are accepted through the Christ, reconciled to God through Jesus' blood, our Father loves and blesses and watches over us for good, even as if we had never sinned.

Indeed, Paul in one place seems to extend the meaning of the word much further. He says, "Not the hearers of the law are just before God, but the doers of the law shall be justified." Here he appears to refer our justification to the sentence of the Great Day. And Jesus unquestionably does, also, when He says, "By thy words thou shalt be justified" (Mt. 12:37). This proves that for every idle word men shall speak, they shall give an account in the day of judgment. We can hardly produce any other instance of Paul's using the word in that distant sense. In the general vein of his writings, it is evident he does not. Least of all does he use it like this in the text before us, which undeniably speaks not of those who have already finished their course, but of those who are now just setting out, just beginning to run the race which is set before them.

"Who Are the Justified?"

The third thing which is to be considered is, who are the justified? The Apostle tells us expressly: the ungodly are justified. God justifies the ungodly, of every kind and degree, and none but the ungodly. As any who are righteous need no repentance, so they need no forgiveness. It is only sinners who have any occasion for pardon. It is sin alone which admits of being forgiven. Forgiveness, therefore, has an immediate reference to sin, and to nothing else. It is our *unrighteousness* to which the pardoning God is merciful. It is our iniquity which He remembers no more.

This seems not to be considered at all by those who so vehemently contend that a man must be sanctified, made holy, before he can be justified, especially those who affirm that universal holiness or obedience must precede justification. Far from it. The very supposition is flatly impossible, for where there is no love of God, there is no holiness, and there is no love of God but from an understanding that He first loved us. This is grossly and intrinsically absurd, contradictory to itself. For it is not a saint but a sinner knowing himself to be a sinner who is forgiven. God does not justify the godly, but the ungodly; not those who are already holy, but the unholy. The condition on which He does this will be considered shortly, but whatever it is, it cannot be holiness. To assert this is to say the Lamb of God takes away only those sins which were taken away before.

It Is the Sick Who Need the Physician

Does Jesus then seek and save only those who are found already? No. He seeks and saves those who are lost. He pardons those who need His pardoning mercy. He saves sinners from the guilt and power of sin—sinners of every kind and of every degree, those who, till then, were altogether ungodly, without the love of the Father. Consequently, in them dwells no good thing, no truly Christian behavior, but all things which are evil and abominable: pride, anger, love of the world, and the genuine fruits of that carnal mind which is at enmity with God.

Those who are sick and whose burden of sin is intolerable are they who need the Physician. These who are guilty and groan under the wrath of God are they who need a pardon. They are condemned already, not only by God, but also by their own conscience, as by a thousand witnesses, of all their ungodliness, both in thought, word, and work. They cry aloud for Him who justifies the ungodly through the redemption that is in Jesus. The ungodly work nothing good before being justified, nothing that is truly virtuous or holy, but do only evil continually. For his heart is necessarily and essentially evil till the love of God is shed abroad in it. While the tree is corrupt, so are the fruits, for an evil tree cannot bring forth good fruit.

The Unjustified Do No Good Thing

Some may object, but a man before he is justified may feed the hungry or clothe the needy. But are these good works? The answer is easy: He may do these, even before he is justified, and in one sense these are good works, good and profitable to men. However, it does not follow these are, strictly speaking, good in themselves, or good in the sight of God. All truly good works follow after justification, and they are therefore good and acceptable to God in Christ because they come from a true and living faith. Therefore, all works done before justification are not good, in the Christian sense, for they do not spring from faith in Jesus Christ, though they may spring from some kind of faith in God. They are not done as God has willed and commanded them to be done. We do not doubt, no matter how strange this may appear to some, that these works have the nature of sin.

Perhaps those who doubt this have not duly considered the weighty reason which is here given, why no works done before justification can be truly and properly good. The argument plainly runs:

1. No works are good which are not done as God has willed and commanded them to be done.
2. No works done before justification are done as God has willed and commanded them to be done.
3. Therefore, no works done before justification are good.

The first proposition is self-evident. The second, that no works done before justification are done as God has willed and commanded them to be done, should appear equally plain and undeniable. We need to consider that God has willed and commanded that all our works should be done in love, in that love to God which produces love to all mankind. However, none of our works can be done in this love while the love of the Father, of God as our Father, is not in us. This love cannot be in us till we receive the "Spirit of adoption, whereby we cry, Abba, Father" (Rom. 8:15). If, therefore, God does not justify the ungodly, then Christ has died in vain, and notwithstanding His death, no one can be justified.

Justifying the Ungodly

But on what terms, then, is one justified who is altogether ungodly? On only one term: faith. He who believes in Him who justifies the ungodly may be justified. He who believes is not condemned, but is passed from death unto life. The righteousness, or mercy, of God is by faith in Jesus Christ to all and upon all who believe. God has set Him forth as a propitiation, through faith in His blood, that He might be just, and, consistently with His justice, the justifier of those who believe in Jesus. Therefore, we conclude, a man is justified by faith, without the deeds of the law, without previous obedience to the moral law, which he could not till now perform. "Do we then make void the law through faith? God forbid: yea, we establish the law" (Rom. 3:31). What law do we establish by faith? Not the ritual law, not the ceremonial law of Moses, but the great, unchangeable moral law of love, the holy love of God and of our neighbor.

The Nature of Faith

Faith in general is a divine, supernatural evidence or conviction of things—things not seen, not discoverable by our bodily senses, being either past, future, or spiritual. Justifying faith implies not only a divine evidence or conviction that God was in Christ, reconciling the world unto himself, but a sure trust and confidence that Christ died for my sins, that He loved me, and gave himself for me. And at whatever time a sinner believes this, be it in early childhood, the middle of his years, or when he is old and white-headed, God justifies that ungodly one. God, for the sake of His Son, pardons and absolves him who had in him, until then, no good thing. God had given him repentance before, but that repentance was neither more nor less than a deep sense of the lack of all good and the presence of all evil. And whatever good he has or does from the moment he first believes in God through Christ faith does not find, but brings. This is the fruit of faith. First the tree is made good, and then the fruit is good also.

I cannot describe the nature of this faith better than in the words of my own church:

> The only instrument of salvation is faith; that is, a sure trust and confidence that God both has and will forgive our sins, that He has accepted us again into His favor, because of Christ's death and passion.
>
> But here we must take heed that we do not stop with God through an inconstant, wavering faith. Peter, coming to Christ upon the water, because he lacked enough faith, was in danger of drowning. So we, if we begin to waver or doubt, will sink as Peter did, not into the water, but into the bottomless pit of hellfire.

Therefore, have a sure and constant faith, not only that the death of Christ is available for all the world, but that He has made a full and sufficient sacrifice for you, a perfect cleansing of your sins, so that you may say with the Apostle that He loved you and gave himself for you. For this is to make Christ your own and to apply His merits unto yourself.

By affirming that this faith is the term or condition of justification, I mean there is no justification without it. He that believes not is condemned already, and so long as he believes not, that condemnation cannot be removed, but the wrath of God abides on him. As there is no other name given under heaven than that of Jesus, no other merit whereby a condemned sinner can ever be saved from the guilt of sin, so there is no other way of obtaining a share in His merit than by faith in His name. As long as we are without this faith, we are strangers to the covenant of promise, aliens from the family of God and without God in the world. Whatever virtues a man may have— I speak of those to whom the Gospel is preached—whatever good works he may do, it profits nothing. He is still a child of wrath, still under the curse till he believes in Jesus.

The Moment of Faith

Faith, therefore, is the necessary condition of justification, its only necessary condition. This is the second point to be observed, that the very moment God gives faith to the ungodly, that faith is counted to him for righteousness. He has no righteousness at all before this, not even negative righteousness, or innocence. But faith is imputed to him for righteousness the very moment he believes. Not that God thinks him to be what he is not. But because He made Christ to be sin for us, that is, treating Him as a sinner and punishing Him for our sins, so He counts us righteous. From the time we believe in Jesus, He does not punish us for our sins, but treats us as though we were guiltless and righteous.

Surely the difficulty of agreeing to this proposition, that faith is the only condition of justification, must arise from not understanding it. It means this much. Faith is the only thing without which none is justified, and the only thing that is immediately, indispensably, absolutely required for pardon. Though a man might have everything else, without faith he cannot be justified. On the other hand, though he appears to lack everything else, if he has faith he is justified.

Think of a sinner of any kind or degree, in a full sense of his total ungodliness, of his utter inability to think, speak, or do good, and his absolute readiness for hellfire. Suppose this sinner, helpless and hopeless, casts himself wholly on the mercy of God in Christ, which indeed he cannot do but by the grace of God. Who can doubt but that he is forgiven in that moment? Who will affirm that more is indispensably required before that sinner can be justified?

The Sole Condition of Justification

Now, if ever there were one such instance from the beginning of the world, and there have been ten thousand times ten thousand, it plainly follows that faith is, in the above sense, the sole condition of justification.

It does not become poor, guilty, sinful people who receive whatever blessings they enjoy to ask of God the reasons of His conduct. It is not appropriate for us to call Him in question, who "giveth not account of any of his manners" (Job 33:13). We cannot demand, "Why did you make faith the condition, the only condition, of justification? Why did you decree that he that believes, and he only, shall be saved?"

This is the very point on which Paul so strongly insists in the ninth chapter of this epistle. The terms of pardon and acceptance must depend, not on us, but on Him who calls us. There is no unrighteousness with God in fixing His own terms—not according to ours, but His own good pleasure. He always may justly say, "I will have mercy on whom I will have mercy, namely on him who believes in Jesus." So justification, then, is not of him who wills, nor of him who works to choose the condition on which he shall find acceptance and forgiveness. Therefore He has mercy on whom He will have mercy, on those who believe on the Son of His love. Those who believe not, he leaves at last to the hardness of their hearts.

The Purpose of Faith

We may, however, conceive one reason for God's fixing this condition of justification. Believing in the Lord Jesus Christ, you shall be saved. This hides pride from man. Pride had already destroyed the very angels of God and had cast down a third part of the stars of heaven. Likewise, in a great measure, pride was there when the tempter said, "Ye shall be as gods" (Gen. 3:5), and Adam fell from his own steadfastness, bringing sin and death into the world. It was, therefore, a wise, worthy God to appoint such a condition of reconciliation for Adam and all his posterity, as might effectually humble and abase them. And faith is peculiarly fitted for this end. He who comes to God by this faith must fix his eye singly on his own wickedness and on his guilt and helplessness, without having the least regard to any supposed good in himself or to any virtue or righteousness whatever. He must come as a mere sinner, inwardly and outwardly, self-destroyed and self-condemned, bringing nothing to God but ungodliness, pleading nothing of his own but sin and misery. Thus it is, and thus alone, when his mouth stops and he stands utterly guilty before God, that he can look unto Jesus as the whole and sole propitiation for his sins. Only thus can he be found in Him, and receive the righteousness which is of God by faith.

According to the Word of God, then, you ungodly ones who hear or read these words, you are vile, helpless, miserable sinners. I charge you before God, the Judge of all, go straight to Him, with all your ungodliness. Take heed you do not destroy your own souls by pleading your own righteousness. Go as altogether ungodly, guilty, lost, destroyed, deserving and dropping into hell, and you will find favor in His sight. Know that He justifies the ungodly. As such, you will be brought unto the "blood of sprinkling" as undone, helpless, damned sinners. Look to Jesus. There is the Lamb of God, who takes away your sins. Plead no works, no righteousness of your own, no humility, contrition or sincerity. To do so is to deny the Lord that bought you. No. Plead singly the blood of the covenant, the ransom paid for your proud, stubborn, sinful souls. Who are you that now sees and feels both your inward and outward ungodliness? You are the ones. I challenge you to become a child of God by faith! The Lord has need of you. You who feel you are fit for hell are fit to advance His glory, the glory of His free grace, justifying the ungodly. Oh, come quickly! Believe in the Lord Jesus, and you, even you, are reconciled to God.

11

John Wesley: A Defense of the Revival

A published letter to the Bishop of London, 1747*

A large number of people have for several years charged me with things I knew nothing about. I have generally thought it my duty to pass over them in silence and to be as one who did not hear. The case is different when a person of your station and character calls me forth to answer for myself. Silence right now might be interpreted as contempt. It might appear like a sullen disregard, a withholding honor from him to whom honor is due, were it only on account of your high office in the church. This is especially true when I consider so eminent a person as you to be under considerable misunderstanding concerning me. Were I now to be silent, were I not to do what was in my power for the removal of those mistakes, I could not have a conscience void of offense toward God and toward man.

*John Wesley, A. M., *A Letter to the Right Reverend the Bishop of London* (London: W. Strahan, 1747) and John Telford, B. A., *The Letters of the Rev. John Wesley, A. M.*, (London: The Epworth Press) v. II, pp. 277–291.

But I realize how difficult it is to speak in such a manner as I ought and as I desire to do. When you published your inquiries under the title of *Observations*, I did not lie under the same difficulty. Because, as your name was not inscribed on that publication, I had the liberty to stand, as it were, on even ground. Now I must always remember to whom I speak. May the God whom I serve in the Gospel of His Son enable me to respond with deep seriousness of spirit, with modesty and humility, and, at the same time, with the utmost plainness of speech, seeing we must both stand before the judgment seat of Christ.

In this, then, I entreat you to bear with me, in particular when I speak of myself just as freely as I would of another man. Please do not term this boasting. Is there not a cause? Can I refrain from speaking and be guiltless? And if I speak at all, ought I not to speak what appears to me to be the whole truth? Do you not desire that I should do this? I will, then, God being my helper. Will you bear with me in my folly, if it is such, with my speaking in the simplicity of my heart?

Charges Against the Field Preachers

Your query begins, "There is another species of enemies who ... give shameful disturbance to the parochial clergy, and use very unwarrantable methods to prejudice their people against them, and to seduce their flocks from them"—the Methodists and Moravians, who "agree in annoying the established ministry, and in drawing over to themselves the lowest and most ignorant of the people by pretenses to greater sanctity."

You remark, "Endeavors have not been lacking.... But though these endeavors have caused some abatement in the pomp and grandeur with which these people for some time acted, yet they do not seem ... to have made any impression upon their leaders."

You add, "Their innovations in points of discipline I do not intend to enter into at present, but to inquire what the doctrines are which they spread"—doctrines "big with pernicious influences upon practice."

Six of these you mention after having premised, "It is not at all necessary to the end of guarding against them, to charge the particular tenets upon the particular persons among them." Indeed, it *is* necessary in the highest degree. For if the minister who is to guard his people, either against Peter Böhler, George Whitefield, or me, does not know what our particular tenets are, he necessarily runs, and fights, as one who beats the air. I will fairly admit which of these belong to me. The indirect practices which you charge upon me may then be considered, together with the consequences of these doctrines, and your instructions to the clergy.

"The first that I shall take notice of," you state, "is the Antinomian doctrine." The second: "That Christ has done all, and left nothing for us to do but to believe." These do not belong to me. I am unconcerned with them. I have earnestly opposed them and never did teach or embrace them.

The Word of God: the Final Authority

"There is another notion," you write, "which we find propagated throughout the writings of those people, and that is the making inward, secret, and sudden impulses the guides of their actions, resolutions, and designs." Thomas Church urged the same objection before. "Instead of making the Word of God the rule of his actions, he follows only his secret impulse." I beg to return the same answer as before. In the whole compass of all language, there is not a proposition which less belongs to me than this. I have declared again and again that I make the Word of God the rule of all my actions, and that I no more follow any secret impulse than I follow Mohammed or Confucius.

Before I proceed, allow me to observe that there are three great errors charged against the Moravians, Mr. Whitefield, and me jointly. In none of which am I any more concerned than in the doctrine of the metempsychosis, the transmigration of the soul! You say it was "not necessary to charge particular tenets on particular persons." It is just as if you were putting a stumbling block in the way of our brethren, laying them under an almost insuperable temptation to condemn the innocent with the guilty. I beseech you to answer in your own conscience before God, did you not foresee how many of your hearers would charge these tenets to me? Did you not design that they should? If so, is this Christianity? Is it humanity? Let me speak plainly. Is it even honest heathenism?

I am not especially concerned with instantaneous justification, as you explain it, "a sudden instantaneous justification, by which the person receives from God a certain seal of his salvation, or an absolute assurance of being saved at the last."

"Such an instantaneous working of the Holy Spirit as finishes the business of salvation once and for all," I neither teach nor believe, and am therefore clear of all the consequences that may arise from that statement. I believe a gradual improvement in grace and goodness—I mean in the knowledge and love of God—is a good "testimony of our present sincerity towards God," although I dare not say it is "the only true ground of humble assurance," or the only foundation on which a Christian builds his "hopes of acceptance and salvation." I think no other foundation can a man lay, than that which is laid in Jesus Christ.

Not Guilty of Sinless Perfection

To the charge of holding "sinless perfection," as you state it, I might likewise plead, "Not guilty," because the one ingredient of it, in your account, is "freedom from temptation." I believe there is no such perfection in this life as implies an entire deliverance from manifold temptations. But I will not decline the charge. I will repeat once more my coolest thoughts upon this subject, and that in the very terms which I did several years ago, as I presume you cannot be ignorant:

What, it may be asked, do you mean by "one that is perfect," or one that is "as his Master"? We mean, one in whom is "the mind which was in Christ," and who walks as He walked. It is a man who has clean hands and a pure heart and is "cleansed from all filthiness of flesh and spirit," one "in whom there is no occasion of stumbling," and who accordingly "does not commit sin." To declare this a little more particularly, we understand by that scriptural expression "a perfect man" (Eph. 4:13), one in whom God has fulfilled His faithful word: "From all your filthiness, and from all your idols will I cleanse you" (Ezek. 36:25). "I will also save you from all your uncleannesses" (Ezek. 36:29). We understand this to be one whom God has "sanctified throughout," in "body, soul, and spirit." It is one who walks in the light, as He is in the light, in whom is no darkness at all, the blood of Jesus Christ His Son having cleansed him from all sin.

This man can now testify to all mankind, "I am crucified with Christ: nevertheless I live; yet not I, but Christ liveth in me" (Gal. 2:20). He is holy, as God who called him is holy, both in life and in all manner of conversation. He loves the Lord his God with all his heart, and serves Him with all his strength. He loves his neighbor, every man, as himself, even as Christ loved us. Particularly, he loves those who despitefully use him and persecute him, because they know not the Son, neither the Father. Indeed, his soul is all love, filled with mercies, kindness, meekness, gentleness, long-suffering. And his life agrees with the full work of faith, the patience of hope, the labor of love. Whatever he does, either in word or deed, he does it all in the name, love, and power of the Lord Jesus. In a word, he does the will of God on earth as it is in heaven.

That is what it is to be "a perfect man," to be sanctified throughout, created anew in Jesus Christ, and to have a heart so all-flaming with the love of God as to continually offer up every thought, word, and work, as a spiritual sacrifice, acceptable unto God through Christ. In every thought of our hearts, in every word of our tongues, in every work of our hands, to show forth His praise who has called us out of darkness into His marvelous light. Oh, that both we, and all who seek the Lord Jesus Christ in sincerity, may thus be made perfect in one.

An Altogether Groundless Delusion

If these are not the words of truth and soberness, point out where I have erred from the truth. Show me clearly where I have spoken either beyond or contrary to the Word of God. But might I not humbly ask you that in doing this, you would abstain from such expressions as these: "If they will but put themselves under their direction and discipline" and "after their course of discipline is once over," as not suitable to either the weight or the subject or the dignity of your character. I expect something more than these loose assertions that this is an "altogether groundless delusion," "a notion contrary to the whole tenor both of the Old and New Testament," or that "the Scriptures forbid all thought of it as vain, arrogant, and presumptuous," that they "present all mankind, without distinction, as subject to sin and corruption during their walk in this world . . . and require no more than an honest desire and endeavor . . . to find ourselves less and less in a state of imperfection."

Is it not from your entirely mistaking the question, not at all apprehending what perfection I teach, that you go on to guard against the same imaginary consequences as you did in your *Observations*?

Surely you never took the trouble to read the answer given in the *Farther Appeal* to every objection which you now bring again! You do not now appear to know any more of my beliefs than if you had never proposed one question nor received one answer upon the subject!

Those Fit for Hell Are Fit for Grace

If your purpose was to show my real sentiments concerning the last doctrine you mention, as one would imagine by your adding, "these are his own words," should you not have cited all my words, at least all the words of that paragraph, and not have mangled it?

I wrote thus:

Saturday, 28 June, 1740

I showed at length, in order to answer those who taught that none but they who are full of faith and the Holy Spirit ought to receive communion:

1. That the Lord's Supper was ordained by God to be a means of conveying to men either preventing, justifying, or sanctifying grace, according to their various necessities.

2. That the persons for whom it was ordained are all those who know and feel that they want the grace of God, either to restrain them from sin, or to show their sins forgiven, or to renew their souls in the image of God.

3. That inasmuch as we come to His table, not to give Him anything, but to receive whatever He sees best for us, there is not previous preparation indispensably necessary but a desire to receive whatever He pleases to give.

4. No fitness is required at the time of communion but a sense of our state of utter sinfulness and helplessness. Everyone who knows he is fit for hell is just as fit to come to Christ, in this as well as all other ways of his appointment.

Misquoted into Heresy

In another letter, I explain myself further on this subject:

I am sorry to find that you still state that, with regard to the Lord's Supper, I also "advance many injudicious, false, and dangerous things, such as:

1. That a man ought to receive communion without a sure trust in God's mercy through Christ." You mark these as my words, but I do not know them.

2. "That there is no previous preparation indispensably necessary but a desire to receive whatever God pleases to give." I include abundantly more in that "desire" than you seem to understand, including a willingness to know and do the whole will of God.

3. "That no fitness is required at the time of receiving communion," leaving out the rest of the sentence, which is "but a sense of our state of utter sinfulness and helplessness. Everyone who knows he is fit for hell is just as fit to come to Christ, in this as well as in all other ways of his appointment." Neither can this sense of our utter sinfulness and helplessness subsist without earnest desires of universal holiness.

And now what can I say? I can hardly imagine you never saw this! If you had, how was it possible you should thus explicitly and solemnly charge me, in the presence of God and all my brethren, when I was not present, with meaning by those

210 / *The Nature of Revival*

words "to set aside self-examination, and repentance for sins past, and resolutions of living better for the time to come, as things no way necessary to make a worthy communicant"?

If an evidence at the bar should swerve from truth, an equitable judge may place the thing in a true light. But if the judge himself shall bear false witness, where then can we find a remedy?

You next come with all your might upon that strange assertion, as you term it: "We come to this table, not to give him anything, but to receive whatever he sees best for us." You say "in the exhortation at the time of receiving, the people are told that they must give most humble and hearty thanks . . . and immediately after receiving, both minister and people join in offering and presenting themselves unto God."

Oh, God! In what manner are the most sacred things here treated! The most venerable mysteries of our religion! What quibbling, what playing on words is here! "Not to give Him anything."—"Yes, to give Him thanks." Oh, my lord, are these the words of a bishop of the church?

Questioning the Value of Church Attendance

You go on, "To the foregoing account of these modern principles and doctrines . . . it may not be improper to add a few observations upon the indirect practices of the same people in gaining proselytes. They persuade the people that the established worship by regularly attending is not sufficient to answer the ends of devotion."

You mentioned this also in your *Observations*. In your fourth query it stood thus: "Does not regular attendance to the public service of religion, paid in a serious and composed way, answer the true ends of devotion?" Allow me to repeat part of the answer then given:

> I suppose by "devotion" you mean public worship, by the "true ends" of it the love of God and man, by "regular attendance to the public services of religion, paid in a serious and

composed way," the going as often as we have opportunity to our parish church and to communion administered there. If so, the question is, "Does this attendance at church produce the love of God and man?" I answer, "Sometimes it does, and sometimes it does not." I myself thus attended them for many years, and yet am conscious myself that during that whole time, I had no more of the love of God than a stone! And I know many hundreds, perhaps thousands, of serious persons who are ready to testify the same thing.

I added, (1) We continually exhort all who attend our preaching to attend all the services of the church. They are now more regular in attendance there than they ever were before. (2) Their attending the church did not, in fact, answer those ends at all till they attended our preaching also. (3) It is the preaching of remission of sins through Jesus Christ which alone answers the true ends of devotion.

The Fitness of the Clergy

Also you charge, "They . . . censure the clergy as less zealous than themselves in the different roles of the minister." For this "they are undeservedly reproached by these noisy itinerant leaders."

I am not conscious of this myself. I do not willingly compare myself with any man, even less do I reproach my brethren of the clergy, whether they deserve it or not. But it is needless to add any more on this subject than what was said over a year ago:

I must explain myself a little on that practice which you so often term "abusing the clergy." I have many times had great sorrow and heaviness in my heart on account of these my brethren. This sometimes causes me to speak to them in the only way which is now in my power, and sometimes, though rarely, to speak of them—of a few, not all in general. In either case I take special care to speak nothing but the truth, to speak this with all plainness and love, and in the spirit of meekness. Now if you will call this "abusing," "railing," or "reviling," you must. But still I dare not refrain from it. I must thus rail and abuse sinners of all sorts and degrees, or else I will perish with them.

No Wine or Meat

You continue, "They value themselves upon extraordinary strictness and severities in life, and such as are beyond what the rules of Christianity require. . . . They captivate the people by such professions and appearances of uncommon sanctity. . . . But that which can never fail of a general respect . . . is a quiet and exemplary life, free from many of the follies and indiscretions into which those restless and vagrant teachers are apt to fall."

By "extraordinary strictnesses and severities," I presume you mean the abstaining from wine and meat, which, it is sure, Christianity does not require. But if you do, I fear you are not thoroughly informed of the facts of the matter. I began to abstain about twelve years ago, when I had no thought of "annoying parochial ministers" or of "captivating any people" by doing it, unless it were the Chicasaw or Choctaw Indians in Georgia. However, I resumed to use of them both about two years later, for the sake of some who thought I made it a point of conscience, telling them, "I will eat meat while the world stands," rather than "make my brother to offend." My physician advised me again to stop eating meat and drinking wine, assuring me, "Till you do you will never be free from fevers." And since I have taken his advice, I have been free, from all bodily disorders, blessed be God. Would to God I knew any method of being equally free from all "follies and indiscretions." But this I never expect to attain till my spirit returns to God.

But in how strange a manner you represent this! What a construction you put upon it—"appearances of an uncommon sanctity" in order to "captivate the people," "pretentions to more exalted degrees of strictness," "to make their way into weak minds and fickle heads," "pretenses to greater sanctity" whereby "they draw over to themselves the most ignorant of the people." If these are appearances of an uncommon sanctity, which indeed might bear a dispute, how do you know that they are only appearances, and that they do not spring from the heart? Suppose these were "exalted degrees of strictness." Are you absolutely assured that we practice them only "to make our way into weak minds and fickle heads"? Where is the proof that these "pretenses to greater sanctity," as you phrase them, are mere pretenses, and have nothing of reality or sincerity in them? This is an accusation of the highest nature.

Passing Sentence Without Proof

If we are guilty, we are not even moral heathens. We then would be monsters, not only unworthy of the Christian name, but unfit for human society. It tears up all "pretenses" to the love of God or man to justice, mercy, or truth. But how is this proved? Or do you read the heart, and so pass sentence without any proof at all? Oh, Bishop, ought an accusation of this lowest kind to be received even by the lowest of the people? How much less can this be reconciled with the apostolical advice to the Bishop of Ephesus. "Against an elder receive not an accusation, but before two or three witnesses" (1 Tim. 5:19)—and those, face-to-face. When it is thus proved, rebuke them who sin before all. You doubtless remember the words that follow, "I charge thee before God, and the Lord Jesus Christ, and the elect angels that thou observe these things without preferring one before another, doing nothing by partiality" (1 Tim. 5:21).

You charge we mislead the people into belief in the high merit of punctual attendance of our performances, to the neglect of the duties of their positions. This is not so. You yourself, in this very *Charge*, have borne us witness that we disclaim all merit, even in really good works.

When you wrote this charge before, in the *Observations*, I openly declared my belief "that true religion cannot lead into a disregard of the common duties and offices of life. On the contrary, true religion leads men to discharge all those duties with the strictest diligence and closest attention. Christianity requires this attention and diligence in all positions and in all conditions. The performance of the lowest offices of life as unto

God is truly serving Christ. This is the doctrine I preach continually." Now, if after all this you will repeat the charge, as if I had not once opened my mouth concerning it, I cannot help it. I can say no more. I commend my cause to God.

"A People Called Methodists"

Having considered what you have advanced concerning dangerous doctrines and dishonest practices, I come now to the instructions you give to the clergy of your diocese.

How awful a thing this is! The very expression carries in it a solemnity not to be expressed. Here is a bishop of the church of Christ, one of the leaders in God's right hand, calling together all the subordinate pastors for whom he is to give an account to God. Now he directs them in the name and by the authority of Jesus Christ, how to make full proof of their ministry, so that they may be pure from the blood of men, how to take heed unto themselves and to all the flock over which the Holy Spirit has made the overseers, how to feed the flock of God which He has purchased with His own blood!

To this end they are all assembled together. And what is the substance of all your instructions? "Revered brethren, I charge you all, lift up your voice like a trumpet! And warn and arm and fortify all mankind against a people called Methodists!"

True it is, you gave them several pieces of advice, but all toward this end. You directed them to "repeat . . . the excellency of our liturgy, as a wise, grave and serious service," to show "their people that diligent attendance to their business is serving God," "punctually to perform both the public services of the church and all other pastoral duties," and to "win the esteem of their parishioners by a constant regularity of life." But all these you recommend as a means to your great end, "the arming and fortifying the people against the Moravians or Methodists and their doctrines."

Is it possible? Could you discern no other enemies of the Gospel of Christ? Are there no other heretics or schismatics on earth? Or even within the four seas? Are there no heathens and no deists left in the land? Or are their errors of less importance? Or are their numbers in England less considerable, or less likely to increase? Does it appear then that they have lost their zeal for making proselytes? Or are all the people so guarded against them already that none of their labor is in vain? Can you answer these few plain questions to the satisfaction of your own conscience?

Seducing the People from Their Lawful Pastors

Have the so-called Methodists already monopolized all the sins and errors in the nation? Is Methodism the only sin, or the only fatal or spreading sin, to be found among the people? Have more than two thousand "ambassadors of Christ" and "stewards of the mysteries of God" no other business than to "guard," "warn," "arm," and "fortify" their people against these? Oh, Bishop, if this engrosses their time and strength, as it must if they follow your lordship's instructions, they will not give an account with joy, either of themselves or of their flock, on Judgment Day.

You seemed in some measure aware of this when you very gently condemned the opinion of those who think the Methodists "might better be disregarded and despised than taken notice of and opposed if it were not for the disturbance they give to the parochial ministers, and their unwarrantable endeavors to seduce the people from their lawful pastors," the same complaint with which you opened your *Charge*. "They give shameful disturbances to the parochial clergy, they annoy the established ministry, using very unwarrantable methods, first to prejudice their people against them, and then to seduce their flocks from them."

Whether we seduce them or not, which will be presently considered, I am sorry you should give any countenance to that low, senseless, and now generally exploded slander that we do it for money. This you insinuate by applying to us those words of Bishop Sanderson, "And all this . . . to serve their own belly, to make a prey of their poor deluded proselytes, for this means the people fall unto them, and thereby they gain no small advantage." You must know that my fellowship and my brother's studentship afford us more than sufficient income for life and godliness, especially for the manner of life we choose.

"We Trust to Have a Clean Conscience"

But do we willingly "annoy the established ministry," or "give disturbance to the parochial clergy"? We do not. We trust to have a conscience void of offense on this point. Nor do we designedly "prejudice their people against them." In this also our heart condemns us not. "But you seduce their flocks from them." No. All who hear us attend the service of the church at least as much as they did before. For this very thing we are criticized as "bigots to the church" by those of most other denominations.

Allow me to say you have mistaken and misrepresented this whole affair from the top to the bottom. I am even more concerned to take notice of this, because so many have fallen into your same mistake. It is indeed, and has been from the beginning, the capital blunder of our bitterest adversaries—though how they can advance it, I see not, without loving, if not making, a lie.

It is not our care, endeavor, or desire, to proselyte any from one man to another, or from one so-called church, from one congregation or society to another. We would not move a finger to do this, even to make ten thousand such proselytes. Our desire is to proselyte from darkness to light, from Satan to Christ, from the power of Satan unto God. Our one aim is to proselyte sinners to repentance, the servants of the devil to serve the living and true God.

If this be not done in fact, we will stand condemned, and not as well-meaning fools, but as devils incarnate. If this occurs, then neither you nor any man beside—let me use great plainness of speech—can oppose and "fortify people against us" without being "found to fight against God."

Stopping Sinners from Rushing into Hell

I will try to set this point in a clearer light. There are, in and near Moorfields, ten thousand poor souls for whom Christ died, rushing headlong into hell. Is Dr. Benjamin Bulkeley, their parochial minister, both willing and able to stop them? If so, let it be done, and I have no place in these parts. I will go and call other sinners to repentance. But if after all he has done, and all he can do, they are still in the broad way to destruction, let me see if God will put a word even in my mouth. True, I am a poor worm that of myself can do nothing. But if God sends, by whomever He will send, His Word shall not return empty. The arm of the Lord is revealed. The lion roars, having the prey plucked out of his teeth. And there is joy in the presence of the angels of God over more than one sinner that repents.

Is this any annoyance to the parochial minister? If so, of what manner of spirit is he? Does he look on this part of his flock as lost because they are found by the Great Shepherd? Bishop, great is my boldness toward you. You speak of the consequences of our doctrines. You seem well pleased with the success of your endeavors against them because, you say, they have pernicious consequences and are big with pernicious influences upon practice, dangerous to religion and the souls of men.

A Cloud of Witnesses

In answer to all this, I appeal to plain fact. I ask once more, what have been the consequences of the doctrine I have preached for the past nine years? By the fruits shall you know those of whom I speak. There is a cloud of witnesses who at this hour experience the Gospel which I preach to be the power of God unto salvation. The habitual drunkard that was, is now temperate in all things. The whoremonger now flees fornication. He that stole, steals no more, but works with his hands. He that cursed or swore, perhaps in every sentence, has now learned to serve the Lord with fear and rejoice unto Him with reverence. Those formerly enslaved to various habits of sin are now brought to uniform habits of holiness.

These are demonstrable facts. I can name the men, with their home addresses. One of them was an avowed atheist for many years. Some were Jews. A considerable number were Papists. The greatest part of them were as much strangers to the form as to the power of godliness.

Can you deny these facts? If these facts are allowed, who can deny the doctrines to be, in substance, the gospel of Christ? "For is there any other name under heaven given to men, whereby they may thus be saved?"

But I must draw to a conclusion. You have without doubt had some success in opposing this doctrine. Very many have, by your unwearied endeavors, been deterred from hearing it at all, and have thereby probably escaped being "seduced into holiness," having lived and died in their sins. The time is short. I am past the noon of life, and my remaining years flee away as a shadow. You are old and full of days, having passed the usual age of man. It cannot, therefore, be long before we shall both drop this house of earth and stand naked before God. On His left hand shall be those who are shortly to dwell in everlasting fire, prepared for the devil and his angels. In that number will be all who died in their sins, including those whom you preserved from repentance. Will you then rejoice in your success? The Lord God grant it may not be said in that hour: "These have perished in their iniquity, but their blood I require at thy hands." I am

> Your dutiful son and servant,
> John Wesley.
> London, June 11, 1747